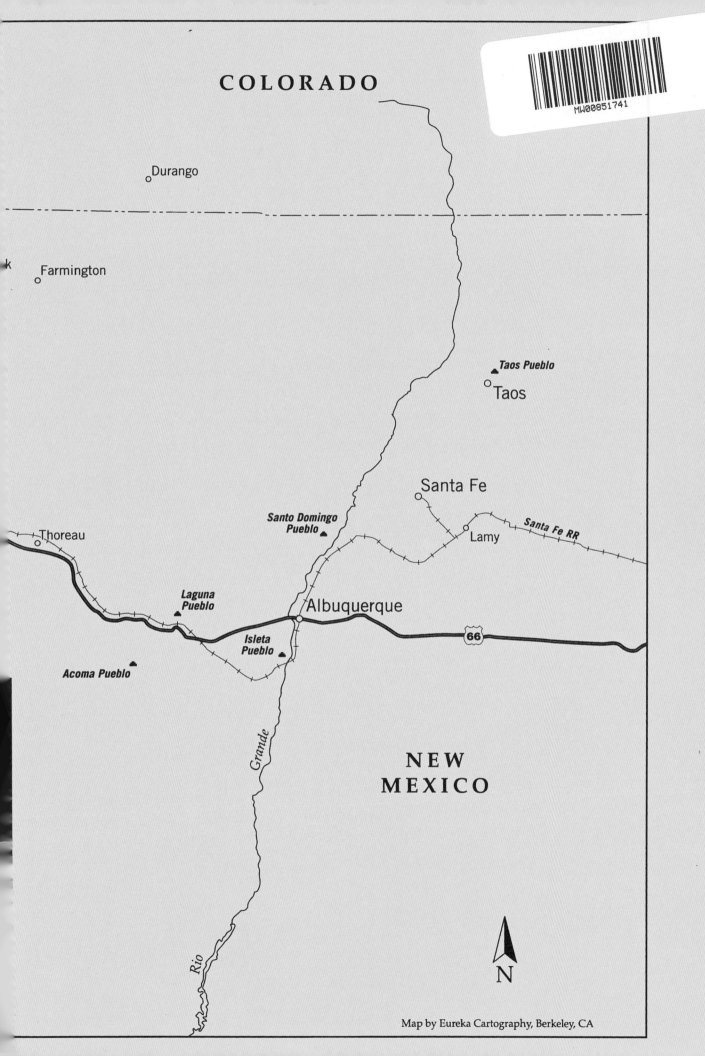

COLORADO

Durango

Farmington

k

Taos Pueblo

Taos

Santa Fe

Santo Domingo
Pueblo

Lamy

Santa Fe RR

Thoreau

Laguna
Pueblo

Albuquerque

Isleta
Pueblo

66

Acoma Pueblo

Grande

NEW
MEXICO

Rio

N

Map by Eureka Cartography, Berkeley, CA

Southwest
Silver
Jewelry

Southwest
Silver
Jewelry

Paula A. Baxter

Schiffer Publishing Ltd

4880 Lower Valley Road, Atglen, PA 19310 USA

Cover photo: Old pawn jewelry. *Courtesy of John C. Hill, Antique Indian Art, Scottsdale, Arizona.*

End sheets: The Four Corners region, showing the major centers for Southwest Native American jewelry production and jewelry trade: 1920s to 1960s.

Library of Congress Cataloging-in-Publication Data

Baxter, Paula A.
 Southwest silver jewelry/Paula A. Baxter.
   p. cm.
 ISBN 0-7643-1244-8
 1. Indians of North America--Jewelry--Southwest, New.
2. Indian silverwork--Southwest, New. I. Title.
 E78.S7 B35 2001
 739.27'089'97079--dc21

                               00-011274

Designed by "Sue"
Type set in UniversityRoman Bd BT/Korinna BT

ISBN: 0-7643-1244-8
Printed in China
1 2 3 4

Published by Schiffer Publishing Ltd.
4880 Lower Valley Road
Atglen, PA 19310
Phone: (610) 593-1777; Fax: (610) 593-2002
E-mail: Schifferbk@aol.com
Please visit our web site catalog at
www.schifferbooks.com

We are always looking for people to write books on new and related subjects. If you have an idea for a book, please contact us at the above address.

This book may be purchased from the publisher.
Include $3.95 for shipping. Please try
your bookstore first.
You may write for a free catalog.

In Europe, Schiffer books are distributed by
Bushwood Books
6 Marksbury Ave. Kew Gardens
Surrey TW9 4JF England
Phone: 44 (0) 20 8392-8585; Fax: 44 (0) 20 8392-9876
E-mail: Bushwd@aol.com
Free postage in the UK. Europe: air mail at cost.
Please try your bookstore first.

This book is dedicated to the Navajo Code Talkers of World War II,
who undoubtedly helped save the life of my father, Edwin S. Baxter,
during his naval service in the South Pacific, 1942-1945.

Acknowledgments

This work could not have been possible without the aid of members of the Antique Tribal Art Dealers Association, Inc., and a number of other dedicated individuals. They have been of invaluable assistance, but are in no way responsible for any errors of fact or omissions: these are the responsibility of the author alone. Special thanks go to Lynn D. Trusdell, New Hope, Pennsylvania, and John C. Hill, Scottsdale, Arizona, for mentoring the initial idea of this book. Contributors to be acknowledged are:

Robert Bauver, Orange, Massachusetts
Steven and Mary Delzio, The Mexican Shack, Somers, New York
Jay Evetts, Gallup, New Mexico
Cynthia and Robert Gallegos, Albuquerque, New Mexico
John C. Hill, Antique Indian Art, Scottsdale, Arizona
Marianne and Robert Kapoun, The Rainbow Man, Santa Fe, New Mexico
Carol and John Krena, Four Winds Gallery, Pittsburgh, Pennsylvania
Martha Hopkins Struever, Santa Fe, New Mexico
Lynn D. Trusdell, Crown and Eagle Antiques, Inc., New Hope, Pennsylvania
William and Sarah Turnbaugh, South Kingstown, Rhode Island
Micky and Dolly VanderWagen, Gallup, New Mexico

Other acknowledgments: Harvey Begay, Steamboat Springs, Colorado; Allison and Mike Bird-Romero, San Juan Pueblo, New Mexico; Ruby Hamilton, Librarian of the National Museum of the American Indian, Suitland, Maryland; Lauris Phillips, South Pasadena, California; Abby Kent Flythe, Fredericksburg, Virginia; David McNeece, The Museum of Indian Arts and Culture, Museum of New Mexico, Santa Fe, New Mexico; Arthur Olivas, Photographic Archives, Museum of New Mexico, Santa Fe, New Mexico; the Indian Arts Research Center, School of American Research, Santa Fe, New Mexico; The Latin American Library, Tulane University; the staff of the Octavia Fellin Public Library, Gallup, New Mexico; Tom Lisanti, Photographic Services and Permissions, The New York Public Library. At Schiffer Publishing, Bruce Waters for photographs of the Trusdell Collection, and Nancy Schiffer for her editorial oversight. Words of gratitude for Elizabeth Diefendorf and the staff of the General Research Division, The Research Libraries, The New York Public Library, and the magnificent Rose Main Reading Room—an oasis of inspiration and a great place to write! And last, but *never* least, to my husband, Barry Katzen, for all the photographs in this book except for the Struever, Trusdell, museum, and institutional illustrations. And for his monumental patience.

Contents

Introduction
Learning from History:
A Century of Influential Jewelry-making

Southwestern Native American jewelry is a truly unique art form. This jewelry, spurred by non-native interest, developed through a cross-cultural exchange that mingled old and new traditions. Within the course of one hundred years, from the end of the Civil War to the socially turbulent 1960s, Navajo and Pueblo peoples devised unique metal and stone adornment. Works from this time period serve as an enduring legacy for contemporary Native American jewelers. This older jewelry is also now a widely recognized and prized commodity. Unfortunately, since the authentic product is in short supply and great demand, it has been subjected to the same kinds of misrepresentation and misappropriation that haunt current native jewelry creation. Those who take time to learn what characteristics make a piece of pre-1970 jewelry a true handmade work of art—or, conversely, a manufactured craft item—gain an assurance that will aid them as buyers or collectors.

The native peoples of the American Southwest had long possessed a tradition of working beads and small ornaments from such natural materials as shell, jet, and turquoise. This tradition was observed by the European explorers who first arrived in the early sixteenth century, and they took note of the jewelry worn by Pueblo inhabitants. European settlers introduced a new tradition, metalsmithing, which had not previously been known in the region. Ornaments made from base metals were created in the early to mid-nineteenth century, but a true reper-

I.1. Group of plain silver bracelets with chisel and file work, mostly Navajo, and demonstrating earliest use of twisted wire, 1880s to 1940s. *Courtesy of Lynn D. Trusdell, Crown & Eagle Antiques, Inc.*

toire of jewelry forms emerged only when silversmithing began in earnest by the late 1860s. Consequently, the fledgling process of Southwestern native jewelry production started soon thereafter with a simple purpose—to provide personal adornment for its peoples. Within twenty years, plain silver jewelry was joined by pieces that featured stones in settings. Traditional pre-conquest forms, such as strings of beads from shell or turquoise, could now be embellished with silver beads or imported glass trade beads. Over the next eighty years, these creative adaptations added detail and variety, enlarging the range of this jewelry into an unique product.

I.2. Group of Navajo concha belts, 1870s to 1920. Center buckle with Lone Mountain turquoise from 1920s. *Courtesy of Robert Bauver.*

I.3. Six Navajo green stone rings and one Zuni ring with deer head design, 1900–1940. *Courtesy of Robert Bauver.*

I.4. Pueblo earrings with large central squash blossom bead flanked by straight trefoil beads, all suspended from a turquoise oval, mid-twentieth century. *Courtesy of Lynn D. Trusdell, Crown & Eagle Antiques, Inc.*

I.5. Two child's necklaces: on left, an early Zuni turquoise petitpoint squash blossom, ca. 1930; on right, a squash blossom necklace with hand-rolled turquoise and small crosses, naja has two tabs on the bottom, and an unusual fastener, 1900. *Courtesy of Lynn D. Trusdell, Crown & Eagle Antiques, Inc.*

I.6. Group of nine cluster work bracelets, mostly Navajo, demonstrating the variety of stone settings used for cluster pieces, 1910s through 1930s. *Courtesy of Lynn D. Trusdell, Crown & Eagle Antiques, Inc.*

Metalworking techniques expanded as well. Native smiths created hand-forged pieces and cast work (with the latter made in molds that were often carved from sandstone or tufa, a local volcanic rock). Access to new and improved tools brought additional creative refinements, because metalsmithing and lapidary processes were made less laborious. When materials for lapidary work became more available—including turquoise from newly opened mines in the region, plus imported coral and white clamshell—technical innovations increased as well. New lapidary techniques often became styles in their own right, based on specific stone shaping and setting (I.6). Changes in design flowered. Some motifs were chosen from preexisting indigenous imagery, such as designs on rock art and old pottery, or on materials uncovered during archaeological excavations in the late nineteenth and early twentieth centuries (I.7). Other designs reflected European-American decorative impulses that were suggested by Indian traders or non-native consumers (I.8). These new designs came from popular imagery seen on mainstream Victorian era jewelry, and depicted motifs such as snakes (traditionally a Navajo taboo) and butterflies.

Eventually, the issue of authentic versus commercial influence became controversial: many non-native people felt a great need to protect what they considered "traditional" Indian arts—even though, ironically, metal jewelry traditions among native peoples of the Southwest were not that old (I.9). In addition, once this jewelry-making was subjected to mechanized processes, Indian arts advocates deplored the inevitable knockoffs and degraded standards that ensued. The commercialization of Southwest native jewelry after 1899 did indeed bring a flood of mass-manufactured imitation Indian goods, including "Indian style" pieces replete with bogus designs. Champions of Indian arts remained suspicious about commercial influences on all subsequent jewelry production; as a result, non-native advocates established the year 1900 as a dividing line, with the nineteenth century considered the time of genuine "antique" native-made jewelry. These people regarded pre-1900 works as "classical" in terms of genuine native artistry and freedom from commercial taint.

I.7. Unusual Hopi pieces with symbols representing rain: earrings ca. 1910–1920; conchas with cottonwood bases and spider silver button design (possibly taken from a kachina carving), ca. 1880s–1890s; mosaic turquoise earrings, ca. 1850s–1880s. *Courtesy of Jay Evetts.*

I.8. Group of jewelry and dress ornaments commissioned by Indian traders for native and tourist use. *Courtesy of Micky and Dolly VanderWagen.*

I.9. Six Navajo *ketohs* (bowguards) showing the range of styles used during the early to mid-twentieth century; most show rectangular X-shape layout. *Courtesy of Lynn D. Trusdell, Crown & Eagle Antiques, Inc.*

I.10. Three Navajo silver boxes with Zuni inlay decoration of Knifewing or supernatural bird deities; accompanying elements include carved wings for figure in the largest box, sun face, lozenges, swastikas, and arrows. *Courtesy of Lynn D. Trusdell, Crown & Eagle Antiques, Inc.*

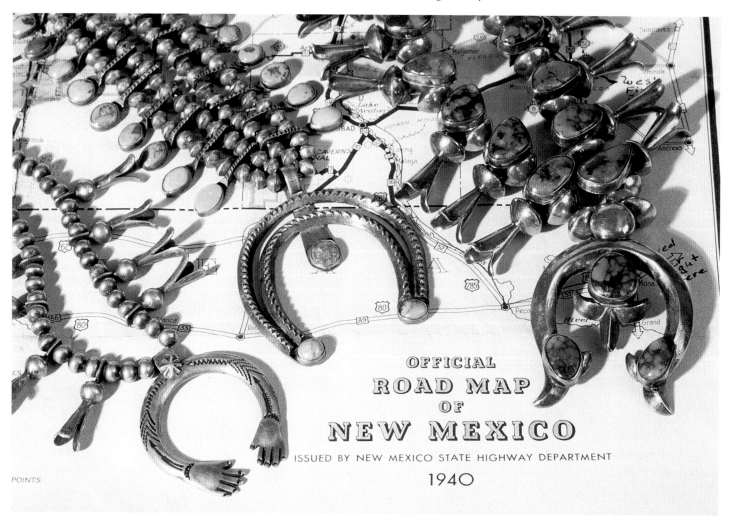

I.11. Three representative Navajo squash blossom necklaces on a tourist map of New Mexico from 1940. *Courtesy of Steven and Mary Delzio.*

Yet another important social force was at work, based also on cross-cultural influence. The century of jewelry-making treated here was largely a time before the achievements of individual native artists were acknowledged. Nineteenth-century European-Americans saw native art production as an anonymous, collective craft effort—and as a form of primitive art. In addition, Indian arts were initially collected as ethnographic evidence of waning or endangered cultures, rather than as evidence of a living art. Since silversmithing by native peoples of the American Southwest was a fairly recent development, it did not register strongly as a relic of material culture. Eventually, a pioneering study by a young anthropologist brought a new perspective. John Adair's *The Navajo and Pueblo Silversmiths*, based on field research conducted in the late 1930s, established a historical context for the adoption and transmission of silver jewelry-making. He interviewed individuals whose recollections reached back to the first generation of native smiths.

Additionally, Indian traders and native arts advocacy organizations actively highlighted jewelers' works in the 1930s and 1940s (**I.12**). By the 1950s, individual silversmiths and lapidarists at last began to receive the type of recognition granted to non-native artists. Two major figures in the history of Native American jewelry, Kenneth Begay (Navajo) and Charles Loloma (Hopi), first gained attention in the 1950s and 1960s for their innovative designs and roles as influential educators.

To provide a better understanding of these critical developments in the evolution of Southwestern Indian jewelry, this book examines the first one hundred years of such work in a chronological fashion. Materials, jewelry forms, techniques (sometimes known as styles), and designs are evaluated decade by decade. Social changes led to innovations in jewelry-making. But the reader should note that while dates for specific technical and stylistic innovations are provided, such dates should be considered warily, and not as absolutes. Documentary evidence is meager for many developments; the history of this jewelry-making is often anecdotal or deductive. This history also emphasizes the role of non-native influence from the 1860s to the 1960s, because this force helped establish the modern Indian jewelry industry. However, while Native American jewelry might be the result of cross-cultural influences, the creative vision of its artists is always predominant. The following pages offer a visual and factual explanation of the process by which this jewelry became a unique art form.

I.12. Three early tourist magazines with information on native
jewelry-making. *Courtesy of Steven and Mary Delzio.*

Chapter 1.
The 1860s:
Metal of the Moon

Upon entering the American Southwest in the sixteenth century, Spanish soldiers observed that the inhabitants possessed certain conventionalized jewelry forms, including beads and pendants. Many of these objects had references back to the works of the Ancient Puebloans, better known as the Anasazi, and other early peoples, including the Hohokam, Mogollon, Salado, and Sinagua (**1.1**). The preconquest Pueblo people mined turquoise and other minerals, and they fashioned adornment from bone, jet, and wood. Shell was available through an extensive trade network, in place by A.D. 1000, that stretched to the natives of the western coast (**1.2**). These early artisans shaped beads from natural materials, and they used an ancient tool, the pump drill, to bore a hole through the bead for stringing (**1.3**, **1.4**). The Europeans did not see any evidence of metallurgical work, although a strong tradition existed in Central and South America. At first Spanish, and then Mexican, settlers brought their own metal ornaments into the region; elaborate silver decorations on clothes and on horse bridles were eye-catching. The natives adopted one or more of these new items, adding them to their original beadwork; as one example, some Indians who converted to Catholicism began to wear small metal rosaries or crosses that were given to them by missionaries (**1.5**).

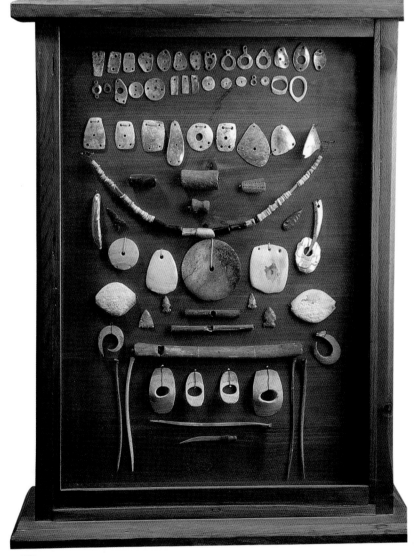

1.1. A display case showing the range of early Hohokam shell ornaments and their transition into jewelry forms. *Courtesy of Lynn D. Trusdell, Crown & Eagle Antiques, Inc.*

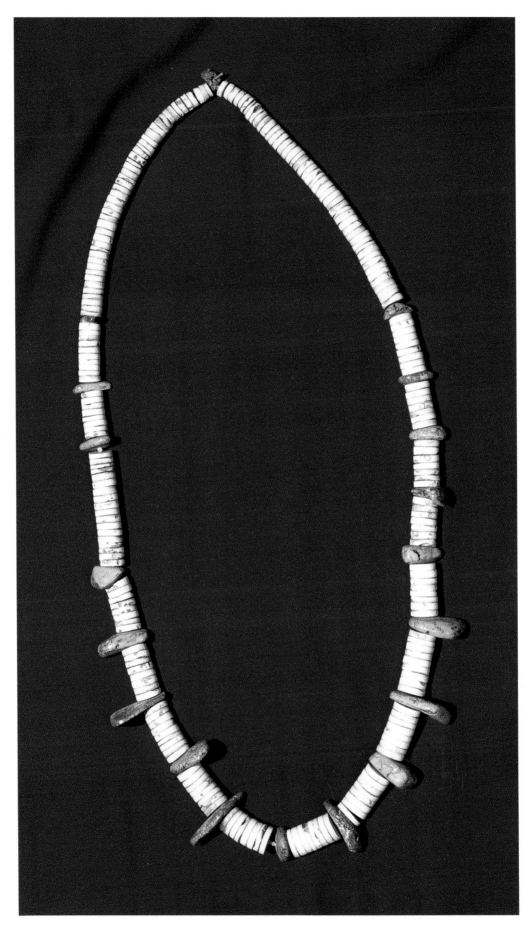

1.2. White shell hand-drilled heishi beads with turquoise tabs, from Zuni Pueblo, ca. 1860s–1870s. *Courtesy of Micky and Dolly VanderWagen.*

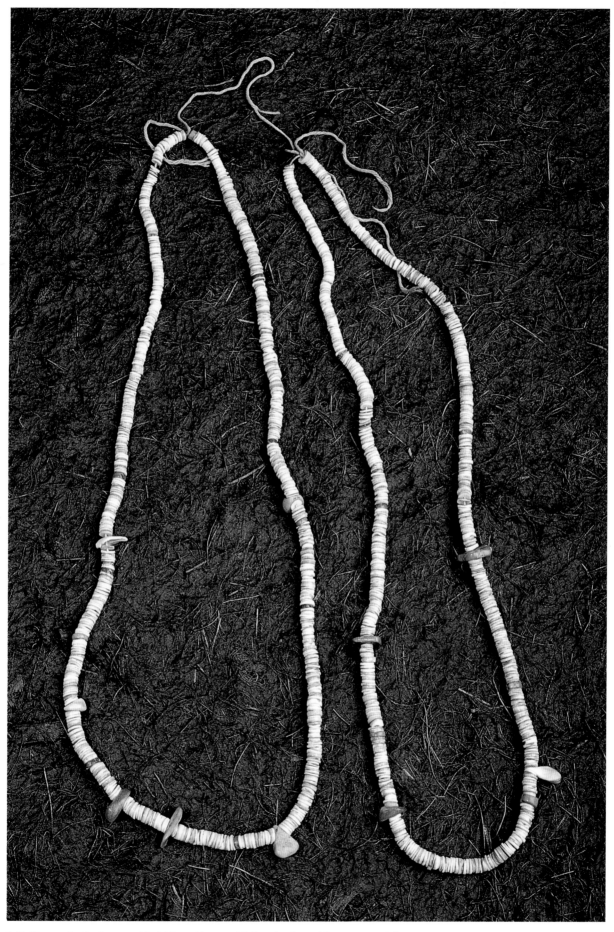

1.3. Two early single strand heishi necklaces with beads shaped by a pump drill, 1840s–1850s. *Courtesy of Lynn D. Trusdell, Crown & Eagle Antiques, Inc.*

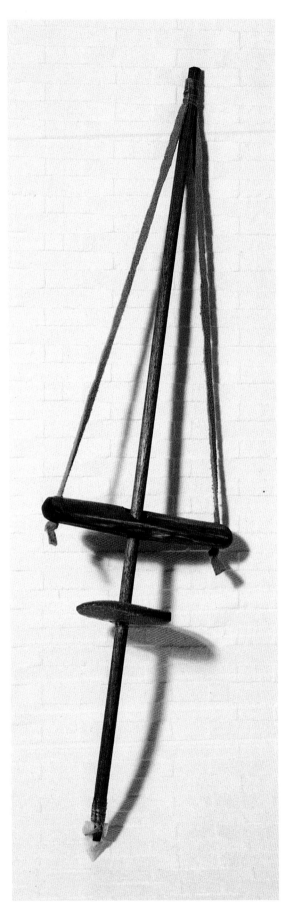

1.4. This pump drill, made as a tourist item (ca. 1960s), shows the construction of the original tool. *Courtesy of Micky and Dolly VanderWagen.*

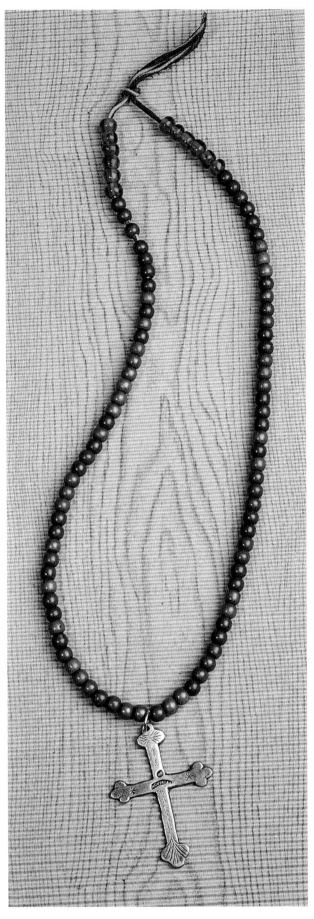

1.5. Cross necklace, probably a trade piece with cross of non-native make: strung with glass beads on top, smaller silver beads on twine, and the silver cross is stamped "Montreal" on its back, Pueblo piece from late nineteenth century. *Courtesy of Lynn D. Trusdell, Crown & Eagle Antiques, Inc.*

Itinerant Mexican blacksmiths and silverworkers (*plateros*) plied their trade throughout the Southwest territory. They often found work at army encampments; Army documents record that Captain Henry L. Dodge brought both a blacksmith and a silversmith to Fort Defiance, Arizona, in 1853. Undoubtedly, some native men learned these crafts by observation. Indians worked iron first, as early as the 1820s, and basic utilitarian items such as buttons, dress sew-ons, and bridle bits were made. Trade with Plains tribes to the north and east brought German silver (a lesser-grade form of silver made from an alloy of copper, nickel and zinc) to the area by the 1830s, but this metal never gained much popularity in the Southwest. Some brass and copper ornaments were made in the 1830s and 1840s. During these same decades, Navajo and Zuni artisans created simple earrings and bracelets from hammered brass and copper wire. But the first reports of native silversmithing date to the mid-1850s; tradition has it that Atsidi Sani was the first Navajo to work both iron and silver at that time.[1]

These activities took place against a background of general conflict, heightened when the United States acquired possession of the region from Mexico in 1848. The new territorial government was anxious to stop the long-running practice of Navajo and Apache raids on settlers. Finally, General James H. Carleton dispatched Colonel Kit Carson to lead troops in the field against the Navajo. The Indians were defeated, and a large group of survivors made the "Long Walk" to incarceration at the Bosque Redondo, near Fort Sumner (in eastern New Mexico), starting in August 1863. As part of the internment, the government attempted to mold the Navajo into farmers, but this experiment failed.

During these difficult years, however, their captors noted that the Navajo possessed one notable talent: they were able to perpetuate a clever mass counterfeiting of metal food ration tickets (**1.6**). More than 3,000 excess tickets were forged before General Carleton had to send to Washington for more intricately designed tokens.[2] When the Navajo were released in June 1868, they returned to their homes with new resolve: they knew that in the years ahead, the material upkeep of the people would mean learning what was necessary for economic survival. Led by twelve designated "chiefs," including such strong figures as Barboncito, Ganado Mucho, and Manuelito, the Navajo began to rebuild.

1.6. Navajo chiefs accused of counterfeiting ration tickets, Ft. Sumner, New Mexico, Bosque Redondo era, 1866. *Courtesy of Museum of New Mexico, Neg. No. 38206.*

In contrast, their neighbors, the Pueblo peoples, had learned to tread more carefully with the American government. Frequently, the Pueblos had sided with the European and American settlers against Navajo raids. Pueblo proximity to established towns kept these peoples careful about retaining their ever-threatened land holdings. Their peaceful cooperation prompted President Abraham Lincoln to present silver-headed canes to the Pueblo governors, which were brought to New Mexico in May 1864 (**1.7**).

1.7. War Chief of Zuni Pueblo. Wheeler Expedition, 1873. Photo by Timothy H. O'Sullivan. *Courtesy of Museum of New Mexico, Neg. No. 41097.*

The indigenous people of the region—Navajo, Pueblo, and others—had admired silver ever since its arrival with the Europeans. Native people, beginning with the Navajo, called it the "metal of the moon" and revered its pale luster. Silver, however, was considered one of the "hard goods," and so it did not possess the same type of spiritual significance given to such materials as turquoise and shell. But while the working of some base metals continued after 1868, silversmithing grew increasingly predominant; by the 1870s and 1880s, some native peoples were calling silver "much nicer looking" than jewelry made from brass.[3] By 1869, Navajo silversmiths were reportedly making buttons from Spanish and Mexican silver coins. Silver bracelets were simple pieces, based on earlier efforts in brass and copper, decorated by fluting, ridging, and twisting the metal. One smith, Atsidi Chon, was believed to have made the first silver concha belt, along with the first silver headstall, at Fort Defiance in either 1868 or 1869.[4] These first belts were devised from Plains-style examples that had large, rounded concha plaques with diamond slots cut in the center. Some basic silverwork techniques adopted at this time included processes for forging silver from cast ingots and creating hand-drawn and hand-forged wire; decoration included finishing with files, cold chisel cutting and stamping, and rocker and scratch engraving.

1.8. Pueblo white shell heishi necklace with Cerrillos turquoise beads, pre-1900. *Courtesy of Jay Evetts.*

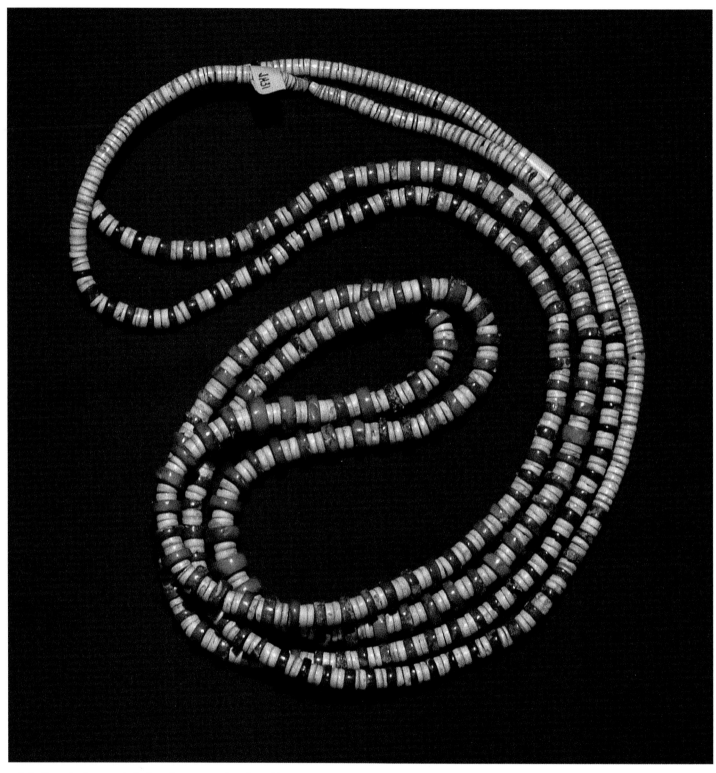

1.9. Two single strand shell and turquoise bead necklaces, Zuni, ca. 1860s. *Courtesy of Micky and Dolly VanderWagen.*

These practices mark 1868 as the starting point for the time period in Southwestern Indian jewelry known as "first phase."[5] The term covers the years between 1868 and 1900, when native silversmithing production expanded in a steady, incremental manner. Works made in this period were intended for local native consumption; these were practical items, such as bridles, saddles, buttons and belts, plus pieces for personal adornment, based on native preferences. Unsurprisingly, jewelry made at this time contains elements that were borrowed directly from Spanish colonial and Mexican ornament. However, by the end of the 1860s, a distinct range of adornment choices emerge, including large-scale beads and pendants with a naja (a crescent form of Moorish origin) or cross shapes. Bracelets with single or multiple bands and hoop-like earrings also appear (**1.11**). These jewelry forms became the basis for a distinctive repertoire that would be repeated throughout the following decades. Such large-sized pendants with beads, concha belts, and solidly made bracelets characterize early Navajo and Pueblo silverwork, and these pieces possessed aesthetic qualities that would be influential for many years to come.

[1] John Adair, *The Navajo and Pueblo Silversmiths* (Norman: University of Oklahoma Press, 1944), p. 3.

[2] For a fascinating account of the Navajo in captivity see Lynn Robison Bailey, *Bosque Redondo: The Navajo Internment at Fort Sumner, New Mexico, 1863-1868* (Tucson: Westernlore Press, 1998).

[3] John Adair, *The Navajo and Pueblo Silversmiths*, p. 4.

[4] Arthur Woodward, *Navajo Silver: A Brief History of Navajo Silversmithing* (Flagstaff: Northland Press, 1971), p. 85.

[5] Larry Frank with Millard Holbrook II, *Indian Silver Jewelry of the Southwest, 1868-1930* (West Chester, PA: Schiffer, 1990), p. 7. The term "first phase" is much used in the antique Indian art market. First phase jewelry is generally considered the most highly prized of commodities; because genuine pieces from this time period are rare and hard to obtain, they are quite expensive.

1.10. Bone hand-drilled beads from pre-contact era, interspersed with buffalo head tabs; restrung as a necklace in the late nineteenth century, and collected from Zuni Pueblo. *Courtesy of Micky and Dolly VanderWagen.*

1.11. Navajo silver bracelet, IAF purchase from the effects of an Indian trader, Durango, Colorado; in his possession since ca. 1887. *School of American Research, Catalog Number S.2.*

Chapter 2.
The 1870s and 1880s:
The Early Years of Silverwork

2.1. Pueblo two-strand necklace with alternating turquoise tabs and shell heishi, 1880s or 1890s. *Courtesy of Lynn D. Trusdell, Crown & Eagle Antiques, Inc.*

It is unclear whether the Navajo or Pueblo worked silver first. Adair, citing his informants, credits the Navajo with this achievement. Other writers, including Charles Lummis, the journalist and author of various books on the Southwest, believed the Pueblo were in the best position to learn the craft first. Whichever viewpoint is the most accurate, the transmission of silversmithing spread fairly rapidly through the region. Atsidi Sani, often credited with being the first Navajo to work silver (sometime in the 1850s), taught a number of fellow Navajos during the 1870s and 1880s; these individuals included his four sons, a brother (or nephew) named Slender Maker of Silver, and several other men. Another smith, Atsidi Chon, has been named as the first Navajo jewelry-maker to set a stone in silver. In 1872 he visited Zuni Pueblo, where he taught silversmithing to a local man, Lanyade; in turn, Lanyade instructed other Zuni men. (Lanyade eventually traveled to the Hopi mesas, where the Hopi learned the craft from him.)

During this time, the Pueblo tradition of beadmaking changed little from its pre-contact era origins during the 1870s (**2.1**). Pueblo artisans painstakingly crafted adornment made from beads of shell and turquoise. These items continued to be traded between the Pueblos and their Navajo and Apache neighbors. Navajo smiths visited pueblos and undoubtedly received strands of beads in exchange for the silver goods they created. Photographs from this time show some native peoples wearing both turquoise-bead necklaces and silver beads with pendants.

The earliest silversmithing techniques were crude due to the lack of available tools. During the 1870s, smiths learned and developed the processes of hammering, annealing, and soldering . Silver solder, in particular, was laborious to make, because granular silver solder involved forging and using a blow pipe. Casting techniques evolved by 1875 (some of the oldest examples of cast work are now found in the Laboratory of Anthropology in Santa Fe, New Mexico). Volcanic tuff, or tufa, which is widely available on the Navajo reservation, was used to create molds for casting. Non-native observers often remarked about Navajo and Pueblo ingenuity, and their ability to "make do" with very rough equipment. Native smiths improvised tools out of discarded materials; they made anvils out of scrap iron or railroad ties, they created potsherd crucibles, and they fashioned goat or sheepskin bellows. Such basic tools meant early decoration was simple, but even designs from the 1870s show evidence of experimentation. Certain jewelry forms such as najas, concha plaques, and manta pins dominate this decade (**2.2**). Crosses and bridles were known to have been made at Isleta Pueblo around 1870. Bowguards, known as *ketohs* (a Navajo word), mounted with silver and plain or domed silver buttons appeared by 1875 (**2.3**, **2.4**). This wrist guard, which protected against the recoil of a bow when arrows were shot, was meant specifically for

2.2. Navajo concha belt, first phase with diamond slot open center, 1870s; buckle from 1910s. *Courtesy of Robert Bauver.*

2.3. Seven Navajo *ketohs,* or bowguards, 1870s to 1930. *Courtesy of Jay Evetts.*

2.4. Detail of four of the earliest *ketohs.* *Courtesy of Jay Evetts.*

native use; as silversmithing techniques grew more elaborate, so did the decorative nature of this object. Bracelets were still simple, either C-shaped cuffs (with the silver having a triangular cross-section) or bands in flat, narrow, or broad widths (**2.5**, **2.6**). Some bracelets were shaped from heavy round twisted wire. German silver pieces, obtained in trade with Plains Indians, influenced some forms (**2.8**).

2.5. Group of plain hand-forged Navajo bracelets, 1890s. *Courtesy of Cynthia and Robert Gallegos.*

2.6. Three Navajo hand-forged thin bangles with cold chisel decoration, 1870s–1880s. *Courtesy of Cynthia and Robert Gallegos.*

2.7. Navajo concha belt, second phase, classic design with closed center, 1880s–1890s; buckle is similar to a *ketoh* design. *Courtesy of Robert Bauver.*

2.8. Two pieces made of German silver, showing the influence of the Plains: left, a pectoral with tin naja (native replacement) and rocker engraving; on right, a round hair plate, 1870s–1880s. *Courtesy of Robert Bauver.*

2.9. Navajo Indian with silver ornaments from U.S. American Ethnology Bureau. Annual Report 2. 1880-1881. *General Research Division. The New York Public Library. Astor, Lenox and Tilden Foundations.*

With its Indian wars largely settled by the 1870s, the United States government began serious exploration of the region's resources; geological surveys, mapping expeditions, and the expansion of mercantile interests (encouraged by the government and the influx of European-American settlers into the area) took place throughout the decade. The steady extension of the railroad into the Southwest brought an increase in freighted goods. Indian traders arrived, ready to open trading posts in areas on, or near to, the Navajo reservation. Charles Crary opened the first trading post in Ganado, Arizona, in 1871. Five years later, Lorenzo Hubbell, soon to become an influential figure, bought this establishment in Ganado; among Hubbell's many activities, he brought Mexican silversmiths to his trading post in 1884, expressly for the purpose of instructing local Navajos. More turquoise became available for traditional jewelry-making (not attached to metal) as new deposits were discovered at mines in Colorado and Nevada during the 1870s, and in Arizona and Texas by the 1880s. The Southwest received increased attention from Easterners through displays at the 1876 U.S. Centennial International Exhibition in Philadelphia.

Anthropologists also began to organize expeditions to the region in order to study Indian culture. In 1879, the year that the Smithsonian Institution's Bureau of Ethnology was established, James and Matilda Stevenson and Frank Hamilton Cushing arrived in Zuni Pueblo, New Mexico. Later, in 1882, Cushing, who had lived as an adopted participant in Zuni pueblo life, brought six Zuni dignitaries on a visit to the East; this event aroused further interest in Southwestern native culture. Throughout the 1880s, metalwork, including some jewelry, was collected on ethnographic expeditions to the region, and these items, along with other artifacts, were brought back to museums in the Midwest and on the East coast. Travel to the Southwest was greatly facilitated by the completion of Atlantic and Pacific Railroad construction in 1882. Indeed, the era of tourism was dawning, marked by the Fred Harvey Company's first hiring of its famous Harvey Girl waitresses in New Mexico in 1883. During the 1880s, certain Indian arts, including jewelry, began to be called "curios." A whole trade developed in obtaining and selling curios; most of the interest in these objects was on their value as articles made and used by Indians. Even at this early date, non-natives collected native-made silver novelties, including powder chargers, tobacco canteens, hair tweezers, and headstalls or bridle bits.

At the start of the 1880s, a black U.S. Army assistant surgeon, Washington Matthews, investigated the work of native smiths while he was stationed at various military outposts in the region, including Fort Wingate, New Mexico. His observations on "Navajo Silversmiths" were published for the *Second Report of the Bureau of Ethnology, 1880-1881* (**2.9**). Matthews, like many other non-natives, was keenly impressed by Navajo ingenuity in making fine silverwork with crude equipment and improvised tools (**2.10**). The native smiths welded or silver-soldered small silver pieces over coal- or charcoal-fired forges. They cut molds from soft sandstone and poured melted ingots into these hollows for casting. Native artisans created their own tongs, cold chisels, and dies, using them in conjunction with purchased iron pliers, hammers, and files. Until they were able to obtain pure borax for flux, Navajo smiths used a local liquid substance called almogen. Matthews noted careful polishing and finishing techniques, including the practice of blanching, or whitening, silver. His report also describes how the Navajo created hollow silver beads from Mexican peso coins. Matthews was particularly interested in the way simple decorative effects were added, noting "These Indians are quite fertile in design."[1]

2.10. Plate of workshop of Navajo smith, from U.S. American Ethnology Bureau. Annual Report 2. 1880-1881. *General Research Division. The New York Public Library. Astor, Lenox and Tilden Foundations.*

2.11. Items showing differences in silver: on right, plain silver naja and chain, 1870s or 1880s; on left, three silver sterling or coin slugs issued to traders, 1930s. *Courtesy of Jay Evetts.*

2.12. Navajo silver buckle, 1870s, originally tied to a Ute beaded blanket strip. *Courtesy of Jay Evetts.*

Native smiths largely used coins to make silver jewelry during these decades (**2.11**). These included U.S. silver dollars and the Mexican peso, which was also called the "dobe dollar." The peso was especially popular through the mid- to late 1880s; because of its lighter metal alloy composition, it was easier to melt and hammer. Coins produced from the peso had a hue that ranged from a silvery white to a yellowish tinge. The luster of the American silver dollar coin was often more blue in tone, and pieces made from these coins could be given a strong, high polish. Items made during this time period, such as beads, buttons, and sew-ons, often show the original coin markings on their undersides, in places where the smith was unable to hammer them out completely (**2.12**). In addition, native smiths still made brass and copper jewelry (mostly bracelets), but the volume of such pieces declined as silver gradually became more plentiful (**2.13**).

Important techniques that were developed in the 1880s permitted more extensive surface decoration. Newly available dies and punches allowed smiths to create additional contrast on silver surfaces. These early tools produced designs that may have been derived from Mexican leather punch work. Another technique, repoussé or repoussage, employed male and female dies to create decoration in relief form, when the back of a metal piece was hammered or pushed through to create a raised design. Repoussé work could be further enhanced by the process of stamping, which makes the relief pattern more prominent. The 1880s saw the first addition of stones to silver jewelry; hand-cut and serrated (sawtooth) mounts, also called bezels,

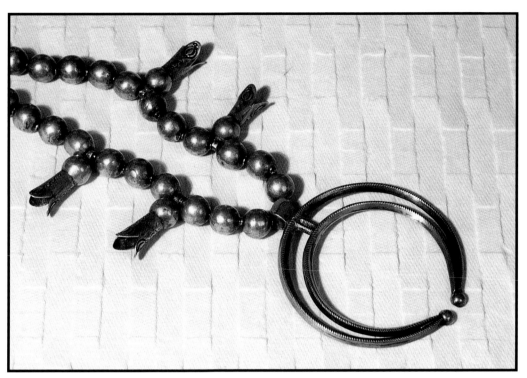

2.14. Pueblo or Navajo squash blossom necklace with large beads and naja, made from hammered silver. Four squash beads are stamped, 1880s. *Courtesy of Robert Bauver.*

2.13. Brass cross made 1870s, placed on silver beads from the 1900s. *Courtesy of Cynthia and Robert Gallegos.*

were shaped onto bracelets and rings. The first stones used, also cut and ground by hand, were small pieces of local garnets, turquoise, malachite, or shell. In the late 1880s, blanching was a preferred finishing process for most Navajo-made silverwork.

2.15. Pueblo or Navajo necklace of hammered silver with large double naja, 1880s. *Courtesy of Robert Bauver.*

2.16. Isleta Pueblo cross necklace with red trade beads, 1880s–1890. *Courtesy of Cynthia and Robert Gallegos.*

34

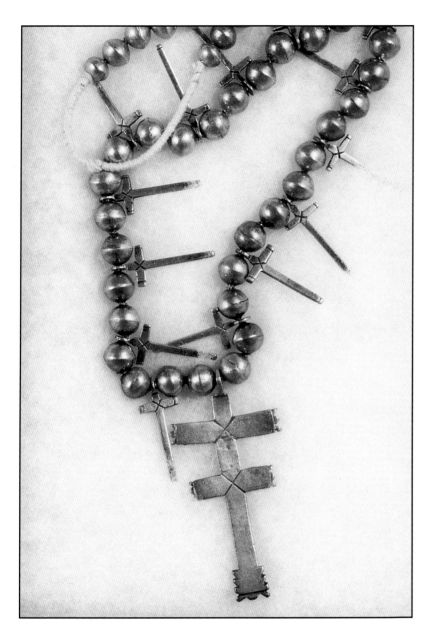

2.17. Silver cross necklace from Acoma Pueblo, 1880s–1890s. *Courtesy of Cynthia and Robert Gallegos.*

Jewelry made by the end of the 1880s was heavy, solid, and somewhat large in scale. Concha belts were marked by round or oval plaques with closed centers, and often were fastened by more elaborately shaped belt buckles. Squash blossom beads (consisting of trefoil-shaped beads added to round beads) appeared on necklaces that averaged around thirty inches in length, and these were frequently anchored with najas or crosses. Pueblo facility with the cross form spawned variations on the design: some of these shapes were of European origin, as in the double-barred French Cross of Lorraine or rosary crosses derived from Spanish religious ornament (2.16, 2.17). The Navajo and Apache revered the cross form as a symbol of the morning star, while the Pueblos often shaped their cruciform versions to resemble the dragonfly, a design that honored the sacred nature of the sun. Blouse ornaments, whether buttons or pins, possessed a greater range of surface decoration, including filed designs of flower and star patterns. By this time, earrings gained a central pendant stone, usually turquoise which was added to the previously plain silver hoop form. The increase of designs on silver pieces reflected native smiths' continuous experiments with stamps, dies, and raised surface relief. Stone settings were added more frequently, but the overall decorative effect remained "quiet and rather inert."[2]

2.18. Navajo naja set with green stone and terminals shaped as hands, ca. 1880-1890. *Courtesy of Jay Evetts.*

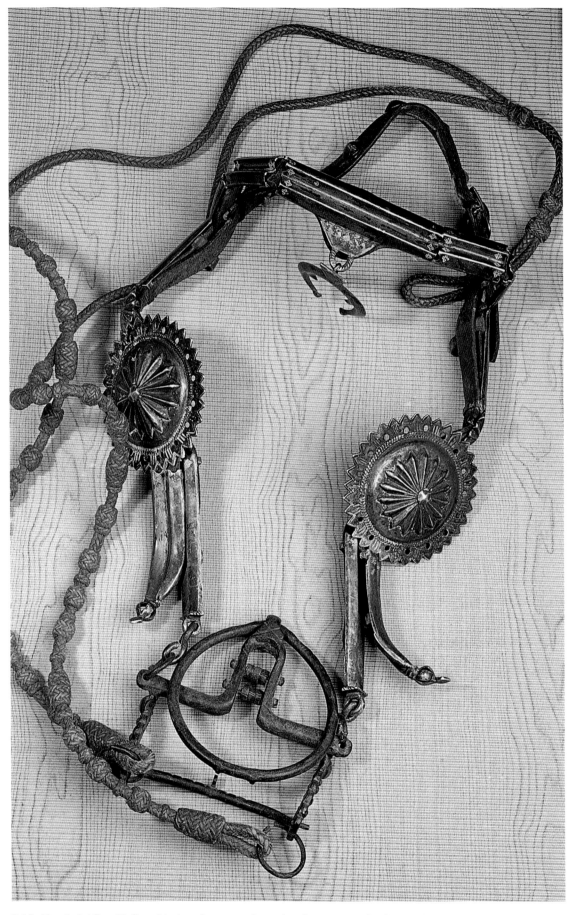

2.19. Navajo bridle with fine chisel work on round concha plaques, metal naja and Mexican braided reins, formerly from collection of William Randolph Hearst, 1890s–1900. *Courtesy of Lynn D. Trusdell, Crown & Eagle Antiques, Inc.*

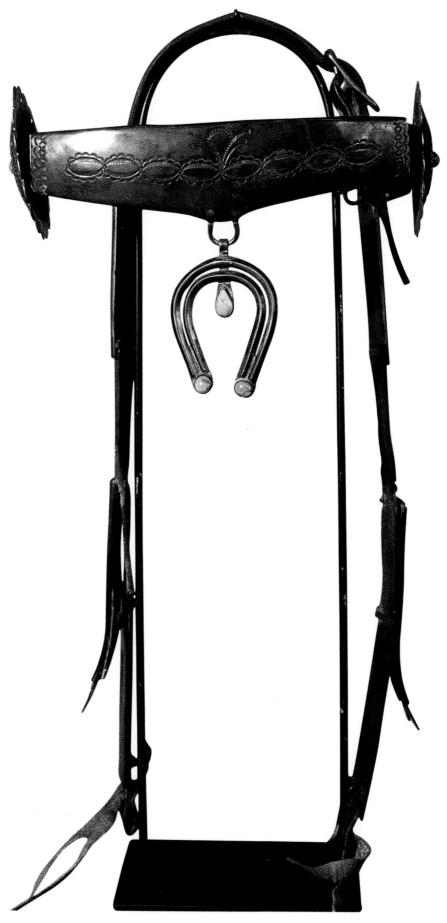

2.20. Navajo bridle headstall, made ca. 1880s–early 1890s; naja added later, possibly ca. 1910. *Private collection.*

2.21. Documented piece made by Navajo smith Slender Maker of Silver for
Chee Dodge, and illustrated in Adair's classic study (1938), made ca. 1880s.
Whole view showing eight trefoils on each side. *Courtesy of Robert Bauver.*

2.22. Detail of naja and immediate beads of Slender Maker of Silver necklace. *Courtesy of Robert Bauver.*

These initial decades of native silversmith production also saw the slow spread of the craft through the region. Atsidi Sani, probably taught by the Mexican smith known as Nakai Tsosi, instructed a number of local men around his home near Crystal, Arizona. His younger brother (or possibly his nephew), Slender Maker of Silver, received much attention for his silverwork, and his creations were praised by Navajo leader Chee Dodge (**2.21**, **2.22**, **2.23**).[3] By the 1880s, smiths working silver had reached Acoma, Laguna, and a few Rio Grande pueblos, such as Isleta and Santa Clara. Outside the Southwest, adornment made and worn by Navajo and Pueblo people began to be recognized as part of their cultural identity. Newspaper accounts and an article in the August 1882 issue of *Century* magazine reproduced portraits of some of the Zuni men Cushing had brought to the East coast. The illustrations showed these individuals bedecked in a rich assortment of silver and stone jewelry (**2.24**, **2.25**). In 1889, Europeans were offered an opportunity to view Southwestern Indian adornment, along with other native arts, at the ethnographic villages of the first world's fair, the Exposition Universelle in Paris.

2.23. Plain silver thin band with file work decoration, attributed to Slender Maker of Silver, 1880s. *Courtesy of Lynn D. Trusdell, Crown & Eagle Antiques, Inc.*

2.24. "Portrait of Na-lu-Tchi, Senior Priest, Order of the Bow...."
The Century 25 (May-October 1882). *Author's collection.*

2.25. "Portrait of Pa-Lo-Wah-Ti-Wa, Governor of Zuni...." *The Century* 25 (May-October 1882). *Author's collection.*

* * *

Viewing these decades as a whole, we see that Navajo and Pueblo jewelry-making traditions now had a chance to commingle. The Navajo have received greater attention for their abilities as silversmiths, but Pueblo contributions were important in their own right. While each group created designs in silver that reflected their own cultural and aesthetic preferences, it was the combination of stone settings on silver adornment that serves as the greatest achievement of this time period. From this time on, silver and stonework would develop along rich artistic lines. These creative choices were the product of native desires. While non-native influence would soon grow strong, the 1880s may be seen as a seminal time for native jewelry design: an established body of jewelry forms distinctively altered by the union of turquoise with silver.

[1]Washington Matthews, "Navajo Silversmiths," *Second Annual Report to the Smithsonian Institution from the Bureau of Ethnology, 1880-81* (Washington, D.C.: U.S. Government Printing Office, 1883), p. 177.
[2]Catherine Chambliss, "Metal of the Moon," *Arizona Highways* 17 (December 1941): 37.
[3]Arthur Woodward, *Navajo Silver,* p. 23. Slender Maker of Silver has become one of the better-known figures among the early Navajo smiths, in part due to a few objects attributable to him, and from the famous photograph of him taken in 1885 by Ben Wittock.

Chapter 3.
The 1890s and 1900s:
The Rise of Commercialism

By 1890, the Mexican peso had become the leading source of silver for native jewelry-making, replacing the now-proscribed U.S. dollar coin. Peso coins were melted into small slugs, producing a solid, lower-grade metal useful for ornamental wear. Both American and Mexican coins continued to be used as decorative elements, often with a copper loop soldered on the back of the coin to attach it onto jewelry; a number of silver bead necklaces were made with coins taking the place of small najas or crosses. While native smiths still made their own dies or stamps by hand, traders now started to import commercial stamps. Indian traders introduced their own favored designs for these stamps, including arrow and swastika motifs. (The swastika image was most likely chosen for its resemblance to the "whirling logs" design used by Navajo medicine men on sandpaintings, and for a similar motif seen on rock art in the region.) Jewelry production still centered around the Ganado, Arizona, and Crystal, New Mexico, areas of the Navajo reservation, but some activities began to move closer to the railroad lines during this period. One of Atsidi Sani's pupils, Long Mustache, was taken to the World's Columbian Exposition in Chicago, where from May to October 1893 he demonstrated Navajo silversmithing. Non-natives of the region and beyond continued to be interested in images (both factual and romantic) of indigenous lifeways. One example of scientific recording can be seen in the work of ethnologist and archaeologist George Hubbard Pepper (1873-1924), who took and collected photographs of Navajo, Hopi, and Zuni Indians and evidence of their material culture (**3.1**, **3.2**).

3.1. A silversmith of Acoma, 1891. *George Hubbard Pepper Collection, Latin American Library, Tulane University.*

3.2. Hopi family. *George Hubbard Pepper Collection, Latin American Library, Tulane University.*

3.3. Group shot of six early Navajo silver bracelets, hand wrought from ingot silver, 1880s to late 1890s. Center bracelet has ray device decoration similar to second-phase concha designs of the same periods. *Courtesy of Robert Bauver.*

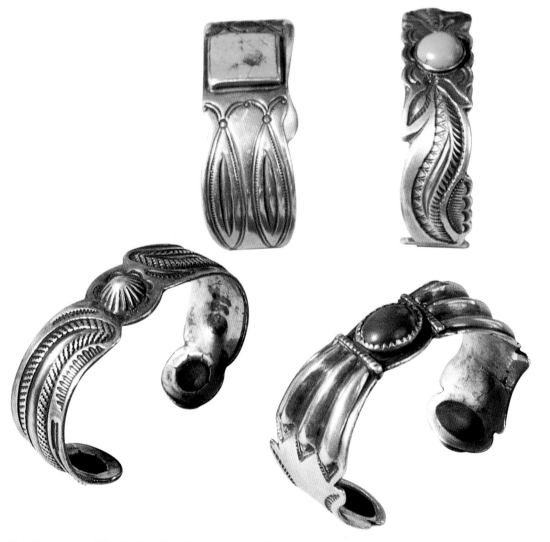

3.4. Four unusual Navajo bracelets showing range of repoussé and stamp work, head-on view. *Courtesy of Robert Bauver.*

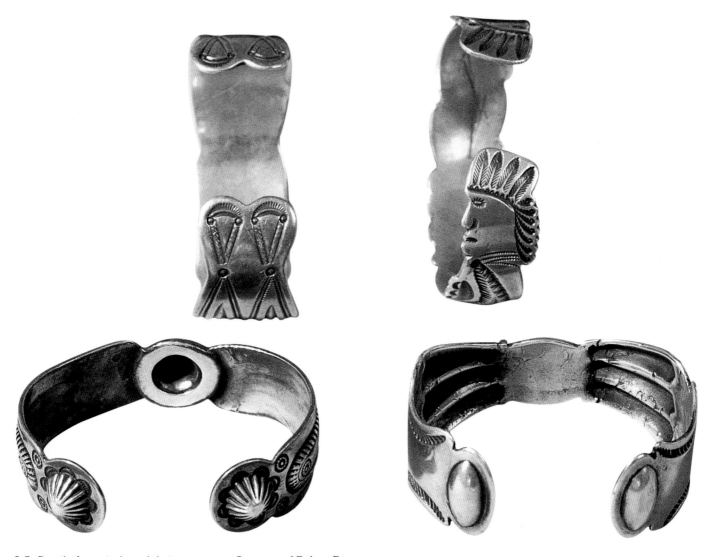

3.5. Detail of terminals and their treatment. *Courtesy of Robert Bauver.*

3.6. Two Navajo bracelets set with stones; single stone originally a drilled bead, 1885–1915; triangular three-stone piece, 1900–1920. *Courtesy of Robert Bauver.*

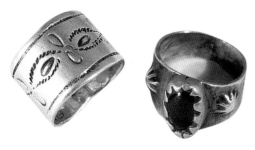

3.7. Two older Navajo rings, one plain silver and the other set with locally found garnet, pre-1900. *Courtesy of Cynthia and Robert Gallegos.*

Silver jewelry made throughout the 1890s still resembled the works created in the previous two decades. However, many of these pieces show a gradual increase in the incorporation of lapidary work. The inclusion of stone settings was clearly a native design choice, and artisans used what materials were available. Turquoise was preferred but often still relatively scarce in supply. Some smiths reused older stones, including drilled beads from ear plugs or necklaces made at an earlier time (**3.6**). Traders were aware of the desire for this significant stone. The Ganado trader Lorenzo Hubbell first imported Persian turquoise in 1895, and other Indian traders looked for different materials. Traders also imported glass trade beads made in eastern and central Europe, and sold them at their trading posts for local usage. Experiments with the effects of colored glass began at this time, with these pieces used as substitutes for turquoise, garnet, jet, malachite, and abalone shell (**3.7**, **3.16**). Through the mid-1890s, single stone settings (or small groups of multiple settings) appeared on rings, bracelets, and as elements inside or at the top of naja pendants. By 1900, new mines opened in the region, and turquoise was more available for use on jewelry (**3.8**). Practical items, such as buttons and sew-ons, continued to be made in both base metals and silver (**3.9**, **3.10**).

3.8. Four bracelets of coin silver, two with animal designs, bull and deer heads, and other stampwork decoration. One bracelet has stone that was originally a drilled earring bead, ca. 1900. *Courtesy of Lynn D. Trusdell, Crown & Eagle Antiques, Inc.*

3.9. Early buttons and sew-ons, Navajo and Pueblo, all pre-1903: collected between 1903 and 1911. *Courtesy of Cynthia and Robert Gallegos.*

3.10. Early silver Navajo buttons, 1890s to 1920s, including legging buttons and sew-ons. Long slender sew-on is made from iron. *Courtesy of Jay Evetts.*

Among the Pueblos, the 1890s served as a critical decade for the transmission of silversmith work. Local men—a few remembered by name—were making jewelry and dress ornaments to suit the tastes of their communities; such pieces often showed a predilection for cross forms, large manta pin shapes, and a more profuse use of turquoise. Jose Rey Leon was making silver at Santa Ana in 1890. Ralph Atencio of Santo Domingo learned the process from a non-native jeweler in Santa Fe around 1893. At Isleta, Jose Jaramillo and Diego Ramos were known to be working silversmiths by 1900. In line with emigration and other social interchanges established during the late nineteenth century, silversmithing came to Hopi from Zuni. Lanyade taught the first smith, Sikyatala of First Mesa, in 1898. Silver creation spread to Second Mesa by 1904 and reached Third Mesa around 1907. Silversmithing often became a family occupation: Sikyatala's nephew, Roscoe Narvasi, was a noted smith on First Mesa by the early 1900s.[1]

3.11. Three manta pins made from nickel silver, 1890s. *Courtesy of Jay Evetts.*

3.12. Three Navajo squash blossom necklaces showing popular styles of the period, 1890–1920; they possess interesting naja terminals, and the piece in the center has added cast attachments on top of the naja. *Courtesy of Robert Bauver.*

3.13. Pueblo composite cross necklace on silver and coral beads, six small crosses and central double-barred cross with huge crescent, ca. 1890–1920. *Courtesy of Robert Bauver.*

The last years of the 1890s—and of the nineteenth century—represent a significant turning point. Most authorities agree that 1899 can be considered the last year for the production of Southwestern Indian jewelry untouched by commercialism. Until then, only a tiny amount of jewelry was made for non-natives, such as for U.S. Army personnel stationed at local forts (**3.14**). But the gradual realization that this jewelry could be an attractive commodity—with a market beyond native consumption—meant changes would be inevitable. American commerce in the Southwest fastened onto ways to exploit the curio appeal of Indian arts (**3.15**).

The Navajo themselves also learned that their jewelry was considered an important item for barter or investment. Natives placed their jewelry "in pawn" as a means of securing loans for other types of goods; these transactions centered around trading posts and stores in reservation border towns. The pawn system meant that many natives had their jewelry held by Indian traders until it could be redeemed. In some cases, the trading post became a place of safekeeping for such "hard goods" until they were needed for wear at a ceremony or social dance. This also meant that non-natives visiting these trading posts had opportunities to admire the silver and lapidary work seen there.

3.14. Two small tobacco canteens made by Navajo smiths for U.S. army officers; piece on left is copper, and smaller canteen on right is silver with file engraved decoration, pre-1900. *Courtesy of Lynn D. Trusdell, Crown & Eagle Antiques, Inc.*

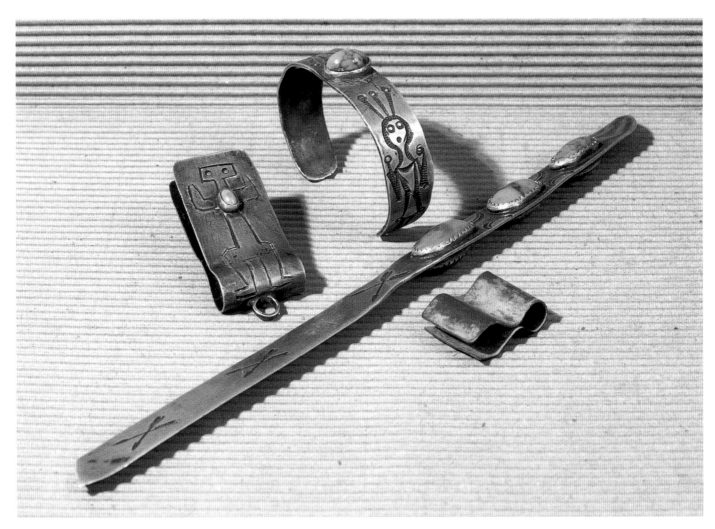

3.15. Early Navajo tourist work, ca. 1900: small tweezers for plucking facial hair, bracelet with figures, letter opener. *Courtesy of Jay Evetts.*

Much of the commercial influence on native jewelry occurred through the Indian traders, who served as willing middlemen for commercially dictated changes; they provided materials and suggestions for local silversmiths. With non-natives seeking adaptations that would encourage further sales of Indian adornment, native accommodation to such interests guaranteed a new form of partnership. Some of the changes instituted to make this jewelry more appealing to non-native consumers included the use of thinner silver (to make the pieces easier to carry and pack), more ornate and obviously "Indian" designs, and a reduction in the size of some forms, such as necklaces. Traders also paid more for work produced according to these new specifications, and native silversmiths created these altered pieces for the sake of economic gain. (And by the early twentieth century, commercialism would inevitably lead to the development of bench production methods, designed to create jewelry more quickly and less expensively than hand-wrought pieces.)

The Fred Harvey Company also played an indelible role in transforming Indian jewelry. Their Indian Department, headed by John Frederick Huckel (1863-1936) and managed by Herman Schweizer (1866-1928), was started in Albuquerque, New Mexico, in 1901. There, the company labored to build a strong inventory of salable Indian products and to increase non-native access to the products. At the Grand Canyon, Harvey Company architect Mary Colter (1869-1958) built Hopi House, which opened in 1905; this handsome tourist attraction served as a place where native artisans demonstrated their crafts. Harvey sold Indian jewelry and various other native-made items there. The Fred Harvey Company was tireless in its promotion of native arts. The company worked with various Indian traders, and also gathered items for major clients, such as William Randolph Hearst, an avid collector of Navajo silver and textiles. Interestingly, at the same time Huckel and Schweizer dictated changes in silverwork meant for tourists, they also seriously collected prime examples of non-commercial silver jewelry. This collection, now at the Heard Museum in Phoenix, Arizona, represents a genuine survey of the finest-quality early Navajo and Pueblo designs.[2]

As a result of these influences, the early part of the new century saw a steady increase in less expensive, souvenir-type objects, mainly rings and bracelets (**3.16**, **3.17**). This coincided with the development of Gallup, New Mexico, a railroad town that became a large mercantile center for such goods. The trader C.N. Cotton launched a mail order catalog—one of the first such marketing endeavors in the Southwest—that advertised specific jewelry pieces for sale. By 1910, a Denver, Colorado, manufacturing firm, H.H. Tammen, was making "Indian style" jewelry. The concept of jewelry handmade by Indian labor was now thoroughly compromised; commercialism had bypassed authenticity for the profit found in mass-manufacturing techniques.

As other manufacturers of souvenir Indian-style goods started up, they would hire natives to work in their shops. However, these Indians rarely supervised the process, despite shop claims that products were "Indian made." Advocates of Indian arts soon became alarmed by such developments. On the other hand, these workshops were training grounds of sorts for some native men who later produced jewelry on their own and trained others as well.

3.17. A group of Navajo silver stamped and hammered bracelets, 1880s to 1920s; bracelet at top collected from Taos Pueblo; fifth bracelet from top may be made from iron; bottom bracelet is nickel with Hubbell glass setting. *Courtesy of Jay Evetts.*

3.16. A group of early Navajo rings, 1890–1910; two at lower left: one with dark Victorian glass and an early example of garnets for ring setting. *Courtesy of Jay Evetts.*

3.18. "Poobitcie—Moqui Girl" from the U.S. Census Office. Eleventh Census of the U.S. *Moqui Pueblo Indians of Arizona.* [Washington: U.S. Government Printing Office, 1893.] *General Research Division. The New York Public Library. Astor, Lenox and Tilden Foundations.*

In contrast, the Pueblo continued to make beads by traditional means, but they now employed some new approaches to bead shapes and lengths (**3.18, 3.19, 3.20**). For those native silversmiths (both Navajo and Pueblo) still creating ornamentation by hand, the 1890s and 1900s brought new and better tools. Access to metalworkers' saws, crucibles, dividers, and tin shears eased the creative process. Traders

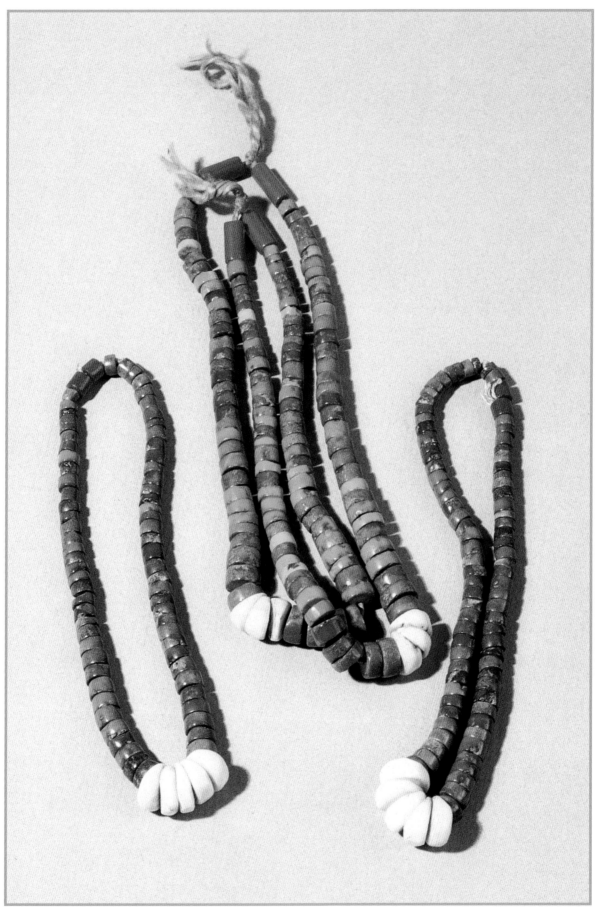

3.19. Two sets of hand-drilled green stone *jaclas* of Pueblo make; they possess white shell "corn" tips and are closed with trade beads, early twentieth century. *Courtesy of Steven and Mary Delzio.*

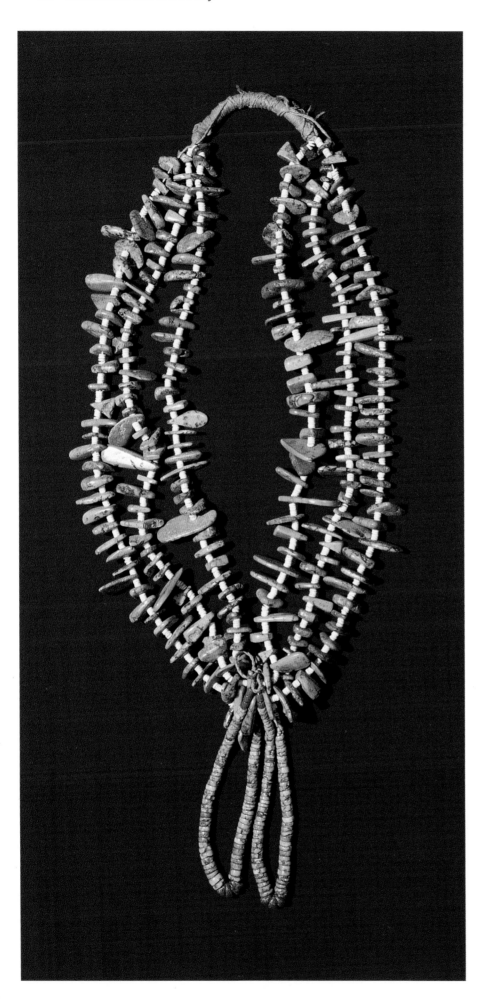

3.20. Three strand turquoise tab and white shell bead necklace presented to Effa VanderWagen in 1898, after she helped nurse many Zunis through a virulent smallpox epidemic in 1897. Necklace beads drilled and strung by Zuni Dick, and piece is tied with two jaclas. *Courtesy of Micky and Dolly VanderWagen.*

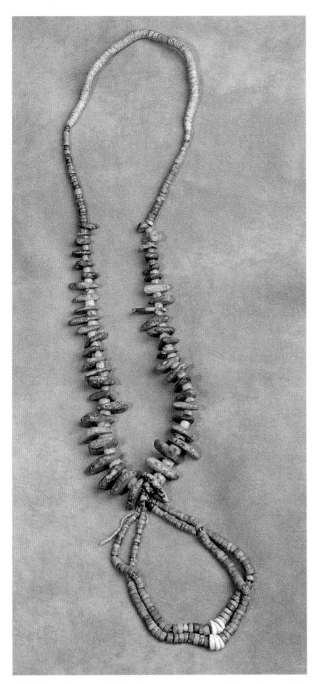

3.21. Single-strand Cerrillos turquoise necklace, in a style sometimes referred to as "medicine man," Pueblo make, late nineteenth century. *Courtesy of Lynn D. Trusdell, Crown & Eagle Antiques, Inc.*

3.22. Pueblo necklace with two pairs of jaclas, with white clam shell heishi, fine quality Blue Gem turquoise, and branch coral, ca. 1900. *Courtesy of Lynn D. Trusdell, Crown & Eagle Antiques, Inc.*

provided commercially cut and polished stones. Commercial solder, tools adapted for doming and shaping, and the introduction of blow-torches made the fabrication of jewelry easier (**3.23**, **3.24**). Decorative touches increased, as in the utilization of hand-drawn wire, small round silver balls (called "raindrops"), and thinner bezel mounts. More commercial stamps were available in a greater variety of patterns, and this led to more intricate designs on silver, including prominent bosses in circles, stars, and lozenge shapes, and keeled or elongated raised surfaces. A wide variety of symmetrical, repetitive markings on silver jewelry is characteristic of fine pre-1910 jewelry, with bracelets often serving as specific examples, along with hand-cut stones set onto silver pieces: the differences in quality between handmade and tourist-style adornment visually signify what would come afterward.[3]

3.23. A set of hand-sharpened dies for jewelry decoration and relief work. *Courtesy of Micky and Dolly VanderWagen.*

3.24. Doming tools used for the creation of beads. *Courtesy of Micky and Dolly VanderWagen.*

3.25. Five Navajo *ketohs,* 1880–1920. Smaller size pieces are of hammered silver and show classic abstract designs. Central *ketoh* (with stone) has outlined details made by rocker engraving. *Courtesy of Robert Bauver.*

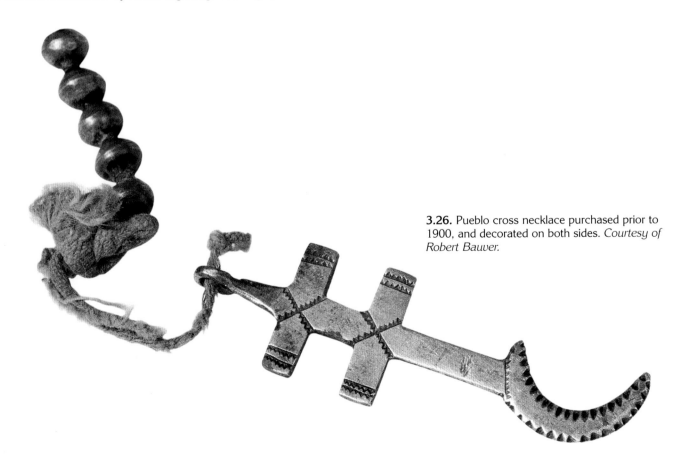

3.26. Pueblo cross necklace purchased prior to 1900, and decorated on both sides. *Courtesy of Robert Bauver.*

3.27. Navajo wide cuff with simple lozenge design, collected late 1890s, and flanked by twin bangles from 1910. *Courtesy of Robert Bauver.*

3.28. Navajo concha belt, ca. 1890; plain style with diamond slots, last concha has stampwork. Buckle may be ten years later. *Courtesy of Jay Evetts.*

3.29. Navajo squash blossom necklace with naja, once owned by Mabel Dodge Luhan, made ca. 1890s–1900. *Courtesy of Jay Evetts.*

3.30. A detail of necklace's beads and trefoil petals. *Courtesy of Jay Evetts.*

3.31. Three hand-forged Navajo bracelets, 1890s–1910; bracelet on left shows hand-filed green stones. *Courtesy of Cynthia and Robert Gallegos.*

3.32. Group of four early rings, pre-1900; stones include: top left, abalone; center, turquoise and red glass; right, jet and turquoise. *Courtesy of Cynthia and Robert Gallegos.*

3.33. Concha belt in the style and period of Navajo silversmith Slender Maker of Silver, 1880s–1890. Belt has seven concha plaques with diamond slots and a butterfly-shaped buckle, showing detail of buckle and one concha. *Courtesy of Lynn D. Trusdell, Crown & Eagle Antiques, Inc.*

Increased elaboration of design can be seen after 1900. However, the essential forms made from 1868 to 1900 remained the same: buttons, concha belts with decorative buckles, bead necklaces, naja or cross pendants, cuff bracelets, and rings with one or more stone settings. Earrings with multiple stones and dangling parts started appearing around 1900. Cast-on work was created for decorative additions to bracelets, bowguards, and belt designs. More elaborate naja designs were made, including triple-bar crescents with twisted wire decoration on the central bars, and additional designs cast or soldered on to the ends of the pendant (3.34). Yet, in spite of this new trend in making jewelry more ornamental in appearance, jewelry production at this time was still limited in numbers.

3.34. Navajo squash blossom necklace with cast triple naja set with a green square stone, six trefoil petals on each side; whole necklace is 32½ inches long, ca. 1890, showing a detail of naja. *Courtesy of Lynn D. Trusdell, Crown & Eagle Antiques, Inc.*

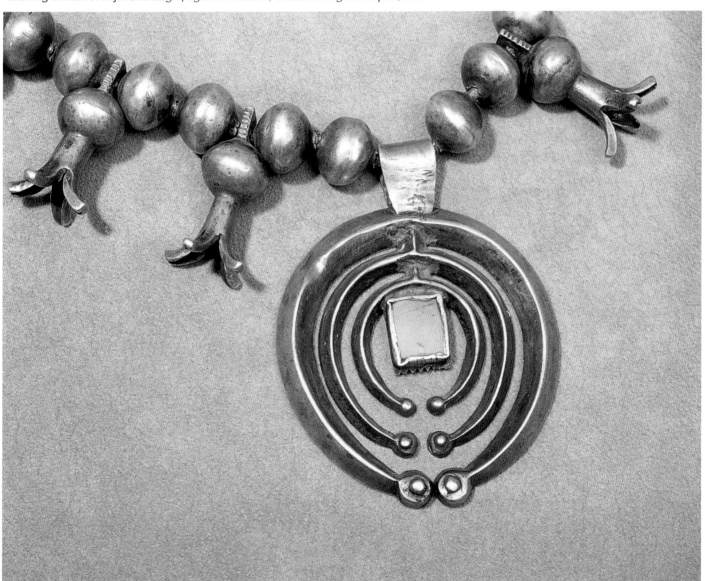

3.35. Ingot silver Navajo bracelet with lozenge design, ca. 1900. *Courtesy of Lynn D. Trusdell, Crown & Eagle Antiques, Inc.*

* * *

Some authorities have called the years after 1900 a "transitional period" in terms of creative emphasis. Attention to mass, proportion, repetitive designs, and decorative contrast continued to be integral to jewelry-making throughout the early twentieth century. In the marketplace, non-native collectors and consumers were being taught that the terms "old pawn" or "dead pawn" (items past the time of claiming by the owner) were also designations for Indian-owned and Indian-worn jewelry made before 1900. Silver might be the predominant feature of a piece, but more and more jewelry was made that combined silver and stones. On occasion, signs of non-Indian aesthetics can be seen; Victorian-era jewelry was "fussy" and very different from the type of work done by Navajo and Pueblo smiths, but some native smiths used increased ornamentation to meet contemporary tastes. In fact, this sort of adaptation was one of the first instances of design experimentation by Navajo and Pueblo jewelry-makers—a process that would continue and flourish in later years. Lapidary abilities, along with the aesthetic enthusiasm for additional stonework, were now being matched to the arrival of better tools. At the same time, mass-manufactured Indian jewelry pieces would permanently join the market in 1910; forty years of hand-wrought silver and stonework had already formed a solid artistic foundation on which to model these manufactured pieces. Impressions of what Southwestern Indian jewelry should look like were further aided during this period by the work of non-native photographers; their attempts to document—and romanticize—Native American lifeways brought more attention to Indian dress and adornment (**3.45, 3.46, 3.47**).

[1]John Adair, *The Navajo and Pueblo Silversmiths*, pp. 176, 194.
[2]See the work of Brian Harvey et al., *White Metal Universe: Navajo Silver from the Fred Harvey Collection* (Phoenix: Heard Museum, 1981).
[3]Larry Frank, *Indian Silver Jewelry of the Southwest*, pp. 7-8. The term "first phase" appears in most literature from the late 1970s on.

3.36. Two wide cuff bracelets with #8 Spiderweb turquoise central square-cut stones; made from ingot silver, with repoussé work and other decoration from button stamp dies, ca. 1900. *Courtesy of Lynn D. Trusdell, Crown & Eagle Antiques, Inc.*

Opposite page:
3.37. Navajo squash blossom necklace of cast and wrought coin silver, bezel folded over the stone; four trefoil beads on each side, one probably a replacement, older style work of the 1890s. *Courtesy of Lynn D. Trusdell, Crown & Eagle Antiques, Inc.*

3.38. Five early silver Navajo *ketohs* (bowguards) showing stamp and chisel work decoration; one piece has coins along sides of wrist ornament, ca. 1900. *Courtesy of Lynn D. Trusdell, Crown & Eagle Antiques, Inc.*

Opposite page:
3.39. Two Pueblo cross pendants: on left, double-barred cross strung on hand drilled shell; on right dragonfly-shaped cross on old Cerrillos turquoise beads, both pre-1900. *Courtesy of Lynn D. Trusdell, Crown & Eagle Antiques, Inc.*

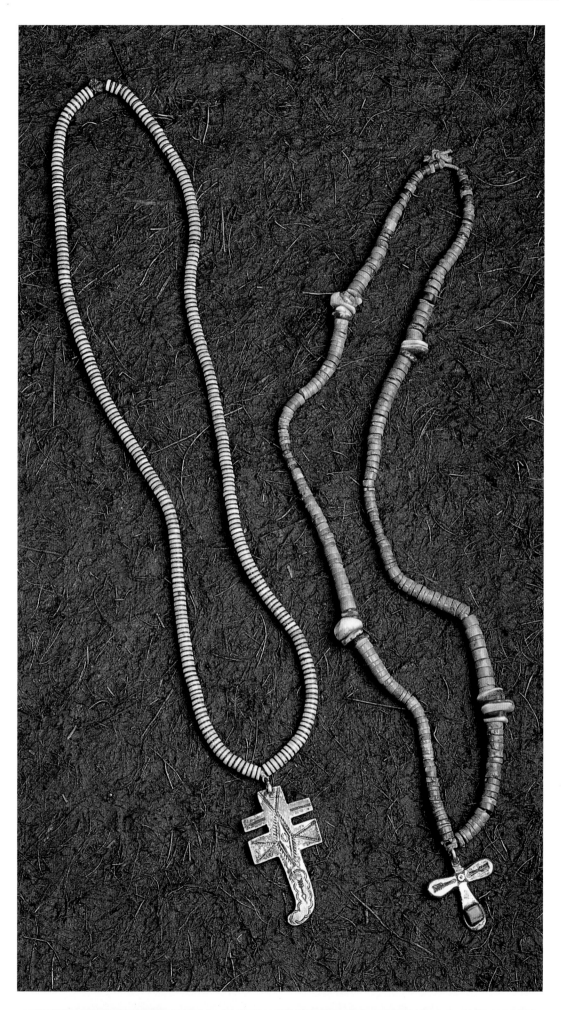

3.40. Double-barred Pueblo cross
necklace; strung with one blue "padre"
bead above the silver cross, ca. 1890.
Courtesy of Lynn D. Trusdell, Crown &
Eagle Antiques, Inc.

3.41. Very fine example of a Navajo plain silver cuff bracelet with stampwork and doming, ca. 1900. *Courtesy of Lynn D. Trusdell, Crown & Eagle Antiques, Inc.*

Below:
3.42. Navajo bridle with headstall, turquoise settings, and plain crescent naja centerpiece made from boar tusk, 1890–1900. *Courtesy of Lynn D. Trusdell, Crown & Eagle Antiques, Inc.*

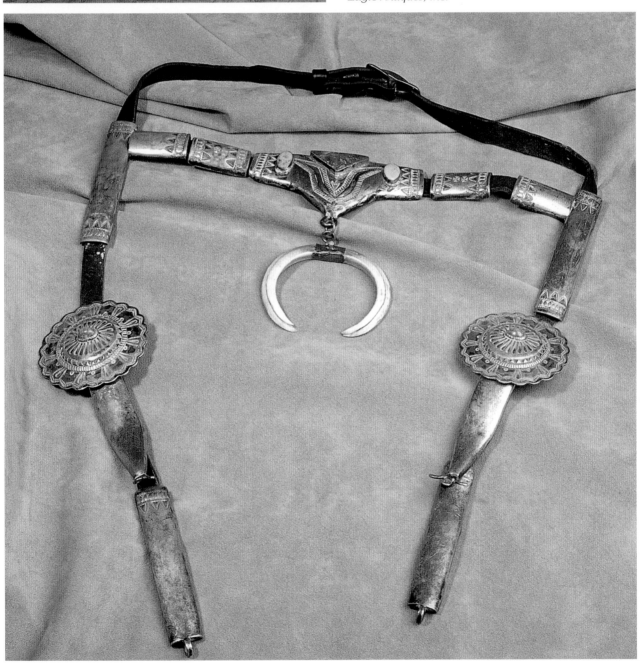

3.43. Twelve older Navajo silver and turquoise rings in a wide range of styles. *Courtesy of Lynn D. Trusdell, Crown & Eagle Antiques, Inc.*

3.44. Plain silver bracelets with abstract designs, center piece has snakes; early Zuni work made during a period when turquoise was scarce, 1900–1910s. *Courtesy of Micky and Dolly VanderWagen.*

3.45. "Zanadolzha—Navajo" from Edward Curtis, *The North American Indian* vol. 1, 1907. *Rare Books Division. The New York Public Library. Astor, Lenox and Tilden Foundations.*

3.46. "Zuni Governor" from Edward Curtis, *The North American Indian* vol. 17, 1907. *Rare Books Division. The New York Public Library. Astor, Lenox and Tilden Foundations.*

3.47. "Pesothlanny" from Karl Moon, *"Indian Studies—Grand Canyon, Arizona.* (1904–1910?)
*Photography Collection. Miriam and Ira D. Wallach Division of Art, Prints and Photographs. The
New York Public Library. Astor, Lenox and Tilden Foundations.*

Chapter 4.
The 1910s and 1920s:
Transition and Expansion

These decades continued to be a "transitional period." By 1910, native jewelry-makers possessed a strongly ingrained sense of design and form. Their creations could be spontaneous in nature, but the influence of European-American culture was now in effect. For better or worse, the opposing tenets of commercialism versus uniqueness (that is, art for art's sake) would affect all future native design. The 1910s and 1920s show strong evidence of adaptation and change. More than ever before, tourism became a potent force in the growing non-native consumer market for Indian jewelry. As a result, jewelry from this time period can be seen for what it had become: more mainstream and modern, incorporating the broadest visual elements of ancestral tradition and contemporary appeal. Again, the mingling of silver with decorative stonework, mainly turquoise but also shell, coral, and stones from the region, would become the focus of creative innovations.

Significant events occurred throughout the 1910s. New Mexico was granted statehood on January 6, 1912, and Arizona achieved the same on February 14. This new status did not aid the states' native peoples—and in fact, statehood even encouraged new encroachments on their land and civil rights. More and more non-natives laid claim to lands that belonged to the natives, and disputes between incoming settlers and local inhabitants increased tensions in the region. In 1915, the Panama-California Exposition held in San Diego opened with a ten-acre exhibition entitled "The Painted Desert." The design team responsible for this display included John Huckel, Herman Schweizer, and Mary Colter, plus the leading museologist and educator Edgar Lee Hewett. A recreated trading post included native smiths in residence, busily demonstrating the making of copper and silver adornment. In 1916, the famed Navajo silversmith Slender Maker of Silver died; his young nephew, Fred Peshlakai, would continue as part of a new generation of influential instructors in the craft. In 1918, the year of America's entry into World War I, Navajo women joined the ranks of practicing silversmiths.[1]

4.1. Group of eight Navajo older style bracelets with a variety of settings, 1900 to 1920. *Courtesy of Jay Evetts.*

4.2. Three pieces set with Hubbell glass: naja and two bracelets, one a single-stone and the other a turquoise cluster style with one glass stone used as part of the set, probably ca. 1920s. *Courtesy of Robert Bauver.*

4.3. Four cluster work bracelets all on heavy silver bands, probably Navajo; these pieces show the increased use of stones in the 1920s as turquoise became more readily available. *Courtesy of Robert Bauver.*

4.4. Five Fred Harvey Company style silver rings, Navajo made, early twentieth-century tourist items with popular designs. *Courtesy of Marianne and Bob Kapoun.*

4.5. A rare jet ring with abalone and red plastic inlay from Santo Domingo, ca. 1920. *Courtesy of Robert Bauver.*

The effects of commercialism had managed to merge the curio status of Indian jewelry with that of other basic commodities. Indian traders and major vendors, such as the Fred Harvey Company, used the preferences of the non-native market to drive specific designs and forms; those items that sold the best were reordered over other styles, so the most popular pieces prevailed over other types of jewelry (**4.4, 4.17**). Traders supplied finished pieces to the vendors, selling silver jewelry by the ounce with additional prices for each stone setting. Even Pueblo beadwork was affected by commercial demand; at Santo Domingo, jewelry-making for tourist sales took on a new importance (**4.11, 4.12, 4.13**) most evident by the 1930s. The formal establishment of the national parks and the National Park Service in 1916 led to new venues for the sale of both authentic Indian jewelry and commercially made imitations. With tourism booming, silversmith production moved closer to relevant outlets, like trading posts and the railroad towns such as Gallup, Winslow, and Flagstaff. The number of mass-production benchwork shops producing Indian-style jewelry and souvenir goods increased: two well-known Albuquerque establishments appeared after 1920: Maisel's in 1924, and Sun Bell in 1935. Pieces made from these shops have their own historical and collectible value today (**4.18**).

4.6. Small three-coin manta pin, made 1910–1915, a common style in contrast to large-scale Zuni manta pins, ca. 1930. *Courtesy of Robert Bauver.*

Left:
4.7. Unusual Navajo cross of silver, hammered with repoussé work, ca. 1915. *Courtesy of Robert Bauver.*

4.8. Naja made from conch shell and inlaid with turquoise, Pueblo, possibly Zuni, ca. 1900–1920. *Courtesy of Robert Bauver.*

4.9. Assorted postcards with views for tourists of native jewelry making and wearing, 1900s to 1920s. *Courtesy of Robert Bauver.*

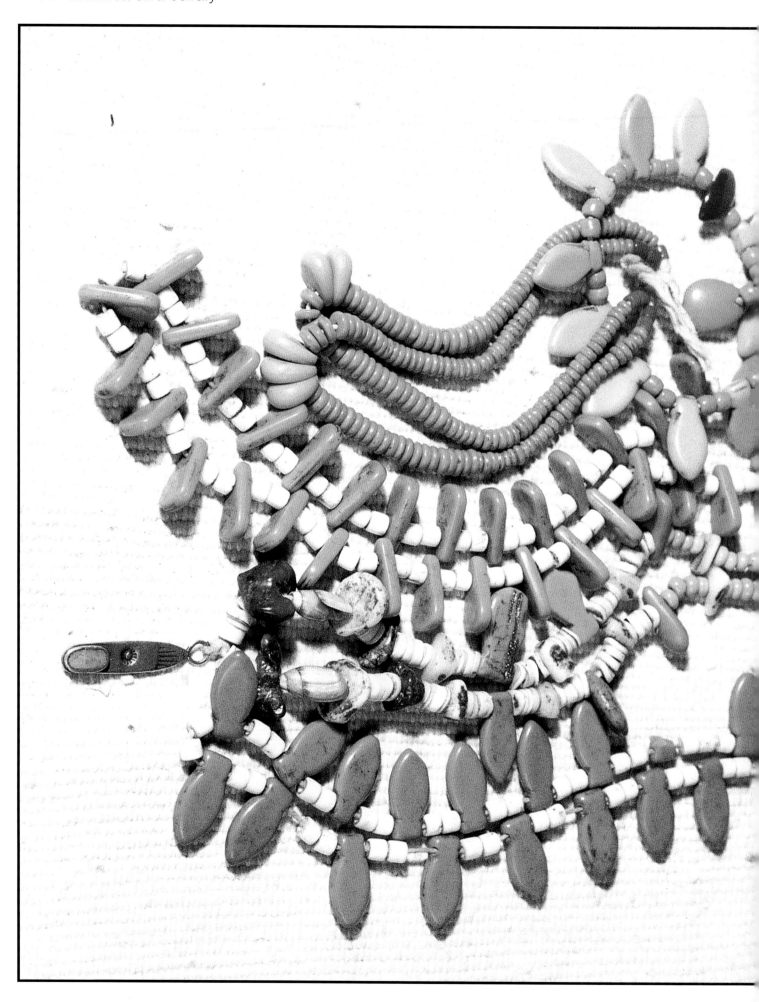

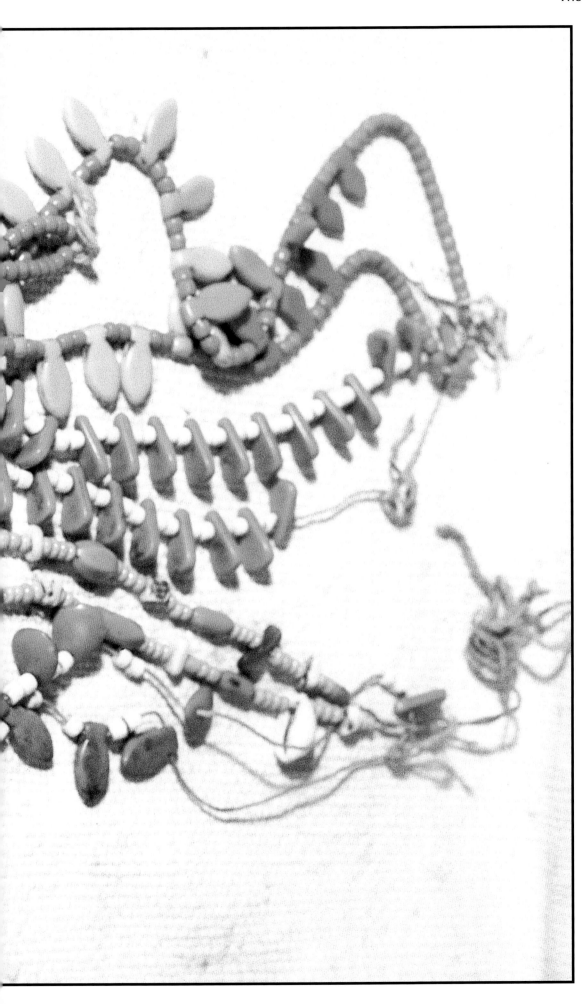

4.10. Four strands of Hubbell glass trade beads in styles of the 1920s and 1930s. *Courtesy of Marianne and Bob Kapoun.*

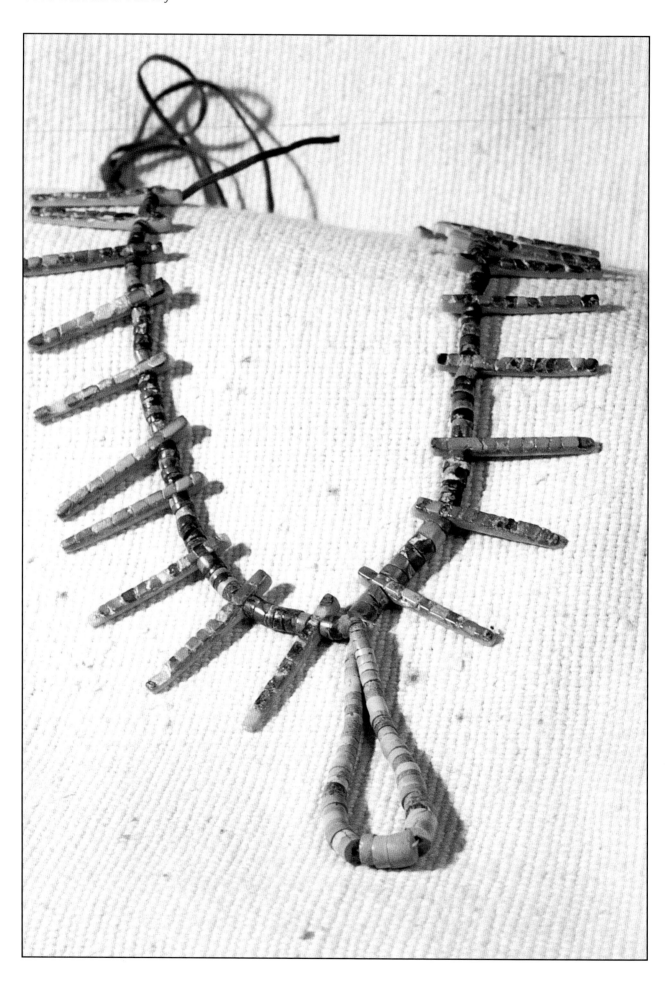

Opposite page:
4.11. Santo Domingo necklace with green
Cerrillos turquoise backed by antler, ca. 1920s.
Courtesy of Marianne and Bob Kapoun.

4.12. Santo Domingo older style tab necklace with thunderbird motif, made with
gypsum, 1920s–1930s. *Courtesy of Marianne and Bob Kapoun.*

4.13. Thunderbird pendant of gypsum, crushed turquoise, and red plastic resin on thick battery casing, Santo Domingo, late 1920s–early 1930s. *Courtesy of Steven and Mary Delzio.*

4.14. Detail showing side view of plastic battery casing. *Courtesy of Steven and Mary Delzio.*

4.15. Navajo silver squash blossom necklace; naja has full hands as terminals and eight trefoil beads, late 1920s. *Courtesy of Steven and Mary Delzio.*

4.16. Two-strand Navajo squash blossom necklace with double crescent naja; fifteen stone tabs on each side, late 1920s or early 1930s. *Courtesy of Steven and Mary Delzio.*

4.17. Commercial Indian style bracelet with popular Fred Harvey Company design, 1920s or 1930s. *Author's collection.*

4.18. Maisel's Indian style tourist bracelet with store hallmark, late 1920s or 1930s. *Author's collection.*

Jewelry designs and alterations to basic forms or shapes went through various evolutions. Zuni-style earrings were increasingly desired by Zuni, Navajo, and Rio Grande Pueblo women throughout the 1910s, thereby setting a precedent for more elaborate multi-part designs to be created (**4.19**). The heishi jacla loop moved from its initial earring form to being placed as well onto bead necklaces as a central pendant (**4.20**). Elaboration was clearly a predominating trend for decorative effect. By the 1920s, the fluted silver bead necklace was devised (**4.21**). Native smiths now used double twisted wire to make filigree-like decorations (undoubtedly a reflection of neighboring Hispanic ornamentation), and leaf forms appeared at some point during this decade. Certain non-native arts advocates criticized these new designs as being derivative and not truly authentic designs. These criticisms were not only accurate, but they also show how resistance to "established" jewelry forms was growing. In the mid-1920s, naja design also became more ornate, with some pieces now showing a closed crescent; a horizontal "oxbow" bar might be placed on the top of the naja. In the late 1920s, the Museum of New Mexico excavated Mogollon sites, yielding a variety of Mimbres Phase (A.D. 900–1150) designs from pottery; these images would be adopted within the next few decades, to be used as a new (yet genuinely old and indigenous) visual vocabulary for silver jewelry.

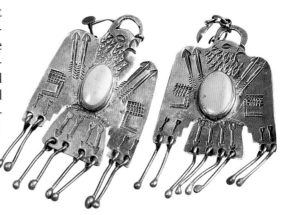

4.19. Thunderbird earrings of a popular tourist design, with stamped arrow decoration, central turquoise, and slender dangles, late 1920s. *Courtesy of Lynn D. Trusdell, Crown & Eagle Antiques, Inc.*

4.20. Necklace made from Bisbee turquoise, double-strand with two jaclas; Pueblo make, with pump-drilled shell heishi, 1915–1920. *Courtesy of Lynn D. Trusdell, Crown & Eagle Antiques, Inc.*

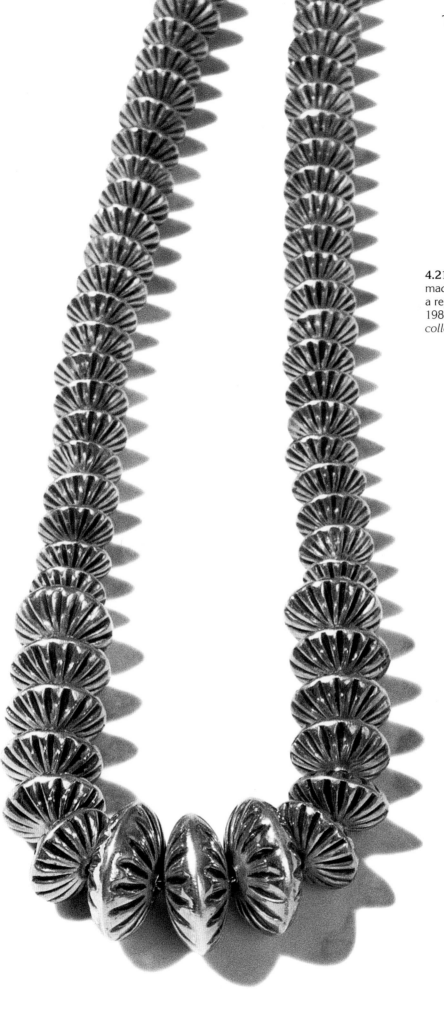

4.21. A fluted silver bead necklace made in the style of the 1920s, but a reproduction piece from the late 1980s-early 1990s. *Author's collection.*

4.22. Navajo rings, all pre-1920, fine examples of early stone settings and bezel work. Ring on top left is a Zuni piece, ca. 1930–1940. *Courtesy of Jay Evetts.*

4.23. Bracelet and two rings set with Hubbell trade glass, ca. 1910. *Courtesy of Cynthia and Robert Gallegos.*

Jewelry-making materials also went through a number of changes during the 1920s. The Mexican government now restricted exports of its coinage as a source for silver. At the same time, commercially made and supplied materials were introduced that eased many previously hand-wrought processes. Bezel strips and varieties of silver wire, including twist and bead wire, could be ordered and stocked. Sheet silver, available in a range of thicknesses, first appeared in the 1920s, but its use became more widespread by the end of the next decade. The last known shipment of turquoise-colored glass trade beads, known generally (if somewhat incorrectly) as "Hubbell glass," arrived from Czechoslovakia in 1923 (**4.23, 4.24**). Other materials arrived and departed in cycles; one example was coral, which could be found in Gallup in the early 1910s but then became scarce until its reappearance there in the 1930s. More turquoise mines opened in the region during the 1920s; the Zuni trader C.G. Wallace purchased newly available turquoise from the Lone Mountain (Nevada) and Villa Grove (Colorado) mines, and had it shipped to Zuni for lapidary purposes.

4.24. Three bracelets set with Hubbell glass; note the simulated matrix markings, Navajo, pre-1920. *Courtesy of Cynthia and Robert Gallegos.*

4.25. Three Navajo bracelets representing important early styles: lower center: carinated piece with stampwork, early raindrops and terminal stones, ca. 1890; on left, hand cut large stone bracelet, 1920s; at right, cast piece with large green stone, finely detailed raindrops, ca. early 1920s. *Courtesy of Lynn D. Trusdell, Crown & Eagle Antiques, Inc.*

4.26. Navajo squash blossom necklace; heavy silver blanched to achieve pale patina, seven trefoil petals on each side and double najas in circle, ca. 1910. *Courtesy of Lynn D. Trusdell, Crown & Eagle Antiques, Inc.*

4.27. Large cuff bracelet in starburst shape of #8 Spiderweb turquoise, with twisted wire and shanks have flattened, heavily stamped terminals, early 1920s. *Courtesy of Lynn D. Trusdell, Crown & Eagle Antiques, Inc.*

More sophisticated equipment for jewelry creation became available in the 1920s, including machines for metal and stone cutting, and the all-important rolling mill—a machine that rolled sheet silver and silver wire into varying gauges, or thicknesses. This instrument did not replace the drawplate, which was used to create wire in a variety of widths, but its use would become essential for studio jewelers. Improvised tools continued to be made, including those incorporating automobile parts, such as pistons and engine rods (**4.28**, **4.29**). By the end of the decade, three large warehouses supplied essential materials and equipment to traders and smiths on the Navajo reservation: the Cotton Company, the Gallup Mercantile Company, and the Kirk Brothers.

4.28. Seven-hole bead punch made from an automotive piston head; such tools were often fashioned from spare machinery parts by blacksmiths in Gallup, New Mexico, early twentieth century. *Courtesy of Micky and Dolly VanderWagen.*

4.29 Female and male stamp dies, with lozenge stamp made from auto crankshaft, mid-twentieth century. *Courtesy of Micky and Dolly VanderWagen.*

This period was an important time for the blossoming of jewelry creation at Zuni. C.G. Wallace had arrived there in 1918, and from the 1920s on he became an active instigator and promoter of their silver and lapidary work. Other traders occupied important roles at Zuni, including the missionary-turned-merchant Andrew VanderWagen. Their combined enthusiasm for Zuni design would boost the pueblo's artistic image in the next decades to come. Zuni jewelry-makers had begun placing an emphasis on stone shaping by 1910. Over the next ten years, they made pieces with more elaborate stone settings and designs. Experimental collaborations between lapidarists and silversmiths marked the start of distinctive Zuni-style inlay and mosaic work. One such collaboration, made between Navajo silversmiths and Zuni lapidarists, led to the creation of the channel inlay technique by 1929. Most inlay done in the 1920s emphasized turquoise, but other materials gained popularity during the mid- to late 1930s. In this manner, the foundations were laid for Zuni's remarkable alliance of techniques (which the creators themselves often termed as styles) and designs, best seen in mosaic inlay work. Zuni silversmiths, including Juan Dedios and Horace Iule, experimented with casting in the late 1910s and throughout the 1920s. Iule has been credited with creating the first silver Knifewing figure for decorative purposes by the late 1920s. The proliferation of Zuni artisans was remarkable: there were only eight silversmiths in Zuni in 1920, but there were already ninety by 1938, when John Adair visited the pueblo.

As Navajo and Pueblo jewelry-making increased through the 1910s and 1920s, non-Indian interest in their creations accelerated as well. Tourism continued to be a major factor as more people were exposed to this adornment. Throughout the 1920s, Southern California's resort status grew. Those visiting or passing through the region had various opportunities to view and purchase native-made ornaments. The Fred Harvey Company displayed its Harvey Collection of high-quality pieces at the Albuquerque Indian Museum in that city's Alvarado Hotel during these decades. Interestingly, officials at the Harvey Company were already reporting difficulties with finding old and rare Indian goods by the mid-1920s.[2] The pawn system was active throughout the 1920s, and tourists would admire the heaps of silver and beadwork on view at these establishments. The market for both contemporary and older Indian jewelry was an established fact, dominated obviously by non-native dealers and traders. Pieces were still billed as curios, but the term "old pawn" was most often employed.

Two events with long-term impact occurred in 1922. The first Southwest Indian Fair took place in Santa Fe, organized by non-native advocates of Indian arts and culture; this event was the forerunner of the annual Santa Fe Indian Market that continues to this day. And on September 25-30, 1922, the first Inter-tribal Ceremonial was held in Gallup; this event soon became another important annual venue (which continues) for the display and sale of native arts, including jewelry. The Gallup Ceremonial, in contrast to the Santa Fe market, was dominated and driven by the mercantile interests of the Indian traders. The 1920s saw other significant developments as well. In 1922, a California couple, Charles de Young and Ruth Elkus, began assembling a collection of Southwestern Indian art that would include remarkable historical examples of silver and turquoise jewelry. And the year 1926 included two other "firsts." The Fred Harvey Company started its Indian Detours on

4.30. Turquoise choker with pieces cut and polished and set in silver on a chain, possibly Zuni, 1920s. *Courtesy of Lynn D. Trusdell, Crown & Eagle Antiques, Inc.*

May 15 of that year, bringing tourists to various locales in their Harvey Cars, accompanied by female guides wearing handsome concha belts, squash blossom necklaces, and other Indian jewelry. Then on November 11, the soon-to-be famous highway Route 66 was officially named and established, running through prime Indian territory (for tourism) in New Mexico and Arizona. The Museum of Northern Arizona, in Flagstaff, was founded in 1928 by Easterners Harold and Mary-Russell Ferrell Colton, enthusiastic supporters of Indian arts. As discussed in Chapter 5, the museum would play a critical role as a venue for quality Indian arts shows and sales, and would have a significant part in the development of Hopi silver jewelry. In 1929, the year of the stock market crash, the Heard Museum was established in Phoenix, Arizona; this museum, too, would gather and promote fine Indian arts.

4.31. Early hand forged naja with green stone, all pre-1890–1910. *Courtesy of Cynthia and Robert Gallegos.*

4.32. Pueblo double-barred cross pendant, ca. 1910. *Courtesy of Cynthia and Robert Gallegos.*

4.33. Classic style Navajo bracelet with twisted wire and lacking stones in setting, 1920s. *Courtesy of Lynn D. Trusdell, Crown & Eagle Antiques, Inc.*

4.34. Navajo row bracelet with alternating triangular and circular stones of Burnham turquoise, stamped design on edges, 1920s. *Courtesy of Lynn D. Trusdell, Crown & Eagle Antiques, Inc.*

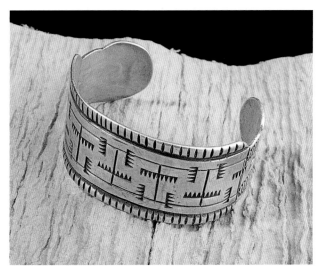

4.35. Coin silver bracelet, Navajo or Pueblo, file decorated in unusual design, 1920s. *Courtesy of Lynn D. Trusdell, Crown & Eagle Antiques, Inc.*

4.36. Heavy sandcast bracelet with central turquoise stone setting, ca. 1920s. *Courtesy of Lynn D. Trusdell, Crown & Eagle Antiques, Inc.*

4.37. Navajo split band bracelet set with old Cerrillos mine turquoise, ca. 1910s–1920s. *Courtesy of Lynn D. Trusdell, Crown & Eagle Antiques, Inc.*

4.38. Navajo bracelet with large square stones, possibly Fox turquoise, late 1920s. *Courtesy of Lynn D. Trusdell, Crown & Eagle Antiques, Inc.*

4.39. Large Navajo wide cuff bracelet with central stone of Blue Gem turquoise; triple shank with appliqué, twisted wire, and raindrops, ca. 1910. *Courtesy of Lynn D. Trusdell, Crown & Eagle Antiques, Inc.*

Right:
4.40. Navajo squash blossom necklace with nine trefoils on each side and domed terminals on naja, 1910s. *Courtesy of Lynn D. Trusdell, Crown & Eagle Antiques, Inc.*

4.41. Coral heishi necklace, tubular beads interspersed with small silver beads on a cotton wrap, probably Pueblo, 1920s. *Courtesy of Lynn D. Trusdell, Crown & Eagle Antiques, Inc.*

4.42. Navajo concha belt of the 1920s; six concha plaques and five butterfly spacers, all plain silver with ridged and scalloped decoration, diamond centers and a multi-lozenged buckle. *Courtesy of Lynn D. Trusdell, Crown & Eagle Antiques, Inc.*

4.43. Three bandelier bags or medicine pouches of Navajo make; most have filed and domed button decorations, 1910s. *Courtesy of Lynn D. Trusdell, Crown & Eagle Antiques, Inc.*

4.44. Two squash blossom necklaces with variant najas, smaller piece is a child's necklace, 1920s; larger necklace's naja has unusual interior center stone, 1910s. *Courtesy of Lynn D. Trusdell, Crown & Eagle Antiques, Inc.*

4.45. Pueblo cross necklace with double-strand beads and heart spacers, early twentieth century. *Courtesy of Lynn D. Trusdell, Crown & Eagle Antiques, Inc.*

4.46. Twisted four-strand coral necklace with mosaic decorated whole shell, Santo Domingo, ca. 1920s. *Courtesy of Lynn D. Trusdell, Crown & Eagle Antiques, Inc.*

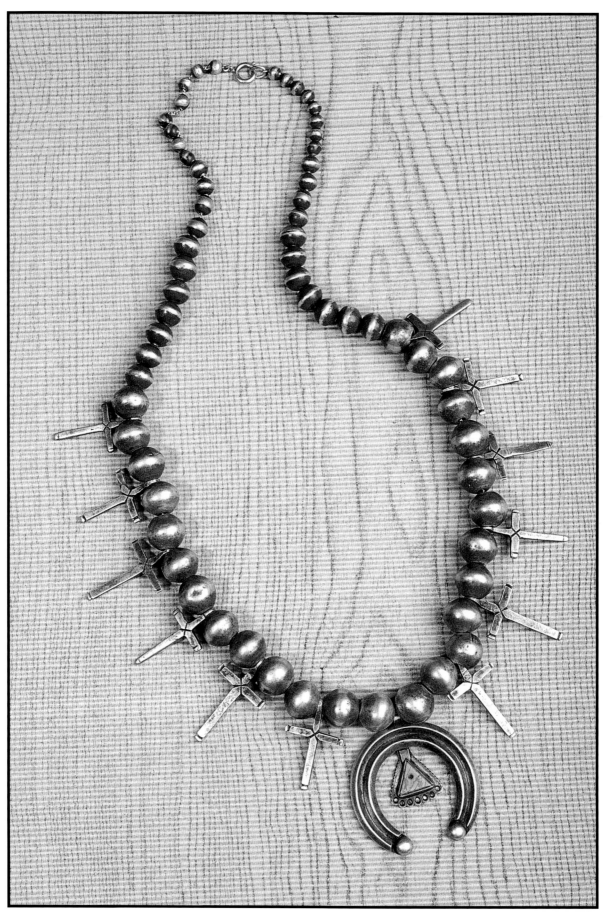

4.47. A child's necklace of silver with naja pendant and attached cross decorations; given by Fred Harvey to a young native friend as a high school graduation present in 1917. *Courtesy of Lynn D. Trusdell, Crown & Eagle Antiques, Inc.*

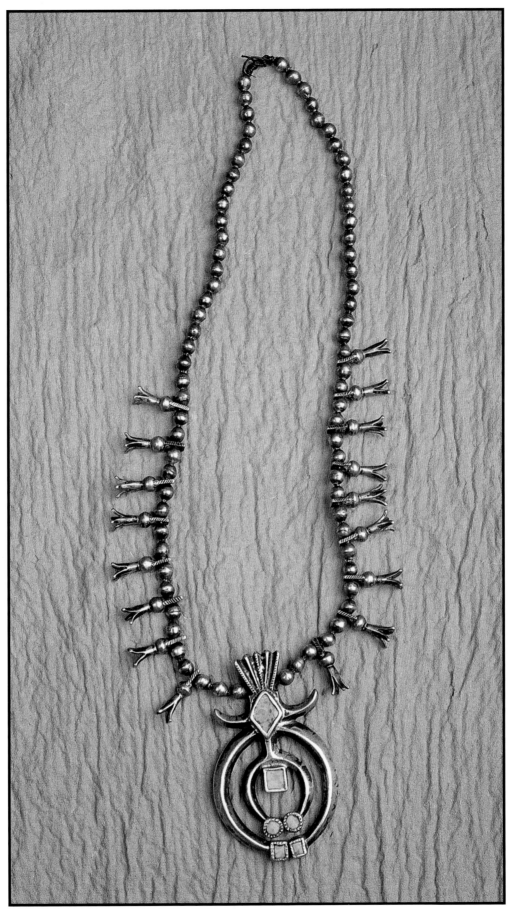

4.48. Squash blossom necklace with elaborately designed naja set with turquoise, pre-1920. *Courtesy of Lynn D. Trusdell, Crown & Eagle Antiques, Inc.*

4.49. Two bird brooches of stamped thin silver, examples of early tourist work; piece on right has more unusual anthropomorphic form, 1910s or 1920s. *Courtesy of Lynn D. Trusdell, Crown & Eagle Antiques, Inc.*

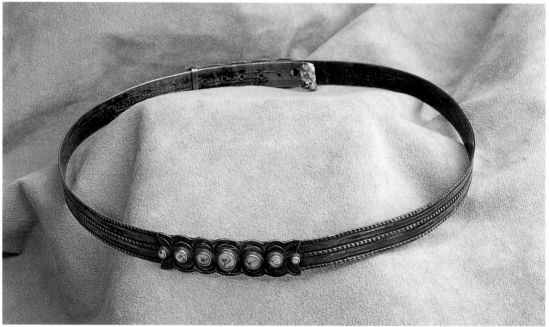

4.50. Navajo silver hatband with seven Blue Gem turquoise stones, 1920s–1930s. *Courtesy of Lynn D. Trusdell, Crown & Eagle Antiques, Inc.*

Opposite page top:
4.51. A traditional style concha belt attributed to Hosteen Goodluck, Navajo, with six conchas and six butterfly spacers on leather, 1920s. *Private collection.*

Opposite page bottom:
4.52. Concha belt with seven plaques and seven spacers, decorated with domed and stamped silver, and turquoise only on the buckle, by Billy Goodluck, Navajo, 1920s. *Private collection.*

By 1930, Southwestern Indian jewelry had achieved a recognizable identity, based on specific forms and designs. While a parallel (and to many minds, bastardized) line of tourist jewelry—which was thinner, cheaper, and highly stylized—competed with the authentic hand-wrought work, the original jewelry was firmly fixed as a desirable commodity. Indian artists themselves, whether smiths, weavers, or potters, had also been transformed into (anonymous) icons of sorts, or as symbols of regional indigenous culture; in many ways, this was the result of the Fred Harvey Company ventures in the Southwest. Visual and verbal portraits abounded, and helped to sell both commercial and handmade works. For example, Charles Lummis, in his popular 1925 book about the wonders of the Southwest, described the jewelry of a Pueblo woman:

> ...silver and coral and turquoise she has abundantly—three or four or half a dozen bracelets of silver and a silver rosary of big hollow beads with alternating crosses and probably a very large pendant; and many strands of costly coral, and ear-rings of silver or of ancient turquoise beads strung in a loop; and perhaps another necklace of old wampum, with markers of spar or conch-shells or turquoise; and many rings of silver, sometimes set with turquoise. [3]

* * *

For some later historians of Southwestern Indian jewelry, the year 1930 serves as a demarcation line. Pieces made prior to this date could be called "antique." Even more revealing, though, was the word now attached to the nature of this older jewelry—"classical." Yet, while some individuals labeled the three decades 1900–1930 as a "transitional period," (with others willing to take the end date up to 1945), there is little doubt that authentic handmade silver and turquoise jewelry made before 1930 possessed a retrospective quality that would prove alluring to Indian arts enthusiasts, museum professionals, and the growing ranks of dedicated collectors.[4] At the same time, signs of innovation, such as the growth of styles based on technical effects at Zuni, are apparent.

[1]John Adair, *The Navajo and Pueblo Silversmiths,* p. 9.

[2]For more information on the Fred Harvey Company and its Indian arts buyers, see Marta Weigle and Barbara A. Babcock, eds., *The Great Southwest of the Fred Harvey Company and the Santa Fe Railroad* (Phoenix: Heard Museum, 1996), pp. 87-101.

[3]Charles Lummis, *Mesa, Cañon, and Pueblo* (New York; London; Century, 1925), pp. 205-206.

[4]See a more thorough discussion of this time distinction, advocated by collectors' literature, in Chapter 8.

Chapter 5.
The 1930s:
Patronage and Partnerships

The year 1930 held a sad note with the death of the influential Indian trader Lorenzo Hubbell, who had worked tirelessly to promote Southwestern Indian arts. Hubbell's last years had been marked by the kind of financial reversals suffered by many businessmen at this time. For the Navajo and Pueblo, the burden of the Great Depression was less immediate, since most natives already lived close to the subsistence level. By the 1930s, however, sales of jewelry had grown increasingly important to the native economy, even though it was still an industry of relatively anonymous artisans. For example, the *Gallup Independent* of August 29, 1931, reported that the trader C.G. Wallace won the best display of new silver at the Gallup Inter-tribal Ceremonial; no native smiths are mentioned by name.

Imitation Indian jewelry had also become plentiful by the start of the decade, and its popularity posed a threat to native livelihoods. Indian arts advocates rallied around various plans to stem the flood of bogus goods. The newly formed United Indian Traders Association (UITA) placed labels on the silver jewelry they sold, stating "Indian Reservation Hand Made" on one side, and "From Solid Coin Silver Slugs" on the other. In 1933, the U.S. Secretary of the Interior banned the sale of imitation Indian arts and crafts in the national parks. Despite all these efforts, prices for Indian jewelry fell in 1936 and 1937 to levels that barely matched the value of the silver used for their creation. Yet, even in the face of these worries, the 1930s can be characterized as a time when creative development continued in the face of adversity.

The persistence of Navajo and Pueblo jewelry creation during this period owes much to two important activities: first, improvements in materials and techniques, and subsequent innovations based on these refinements; and second, a partnership between traders and smiths to facilitate the production of salable goods. For example, sheet silver was now in wider use; from 1932 on, most native smiths used one-ounce sterling slugs made from refineries in the Los Angeles area. The use of coins for silver faded away certainly no later than 1938 in the face of these newer (and more malleable) materials. At the same time, machine-made nickel-plate jewelry increased, clearly for economic reasons. Traders now stocked commercially pre-cut and polished stones for lapidary setting; these included agate, jasper, lapis, and petrified wood. Coral was available (used mostly in the branch-shaped form it had when taken from the waters of the Gulf of California) up to the middle of the decade, before becoming scarce again until the early 1950s.

Smiths and lapidarists reused older materials or sought creative substitutions (**5.1**, **5.31**). Such ingenuity became an emblem of Santo Domingo, where jewelry-makers made thunderbird pendants that were famous with tourists; these, along with other items, made the pueblo noted for its Depression-era jewelry (**5.3**, **5.32**). The pendants were often inlaid with a variety of clever alternative materials; in place of jet and abalone, such unusual materials as automotive battery casings, phonograph record plastic, piano keys, and toothbrush handles were used.

5.1. A late 1930s bracelet with glass cabochon backed by colored tin foil for sparkle effect, and matching ring, probably Navajo. *Courtesy of Marianne and Bob Kapoun.*

5.2. Navajo agate picture stone bracelet, late 1930s, and small ring set with petrified wood, 1940s. *Courtesy of Marianne and Bob Kapoun.*

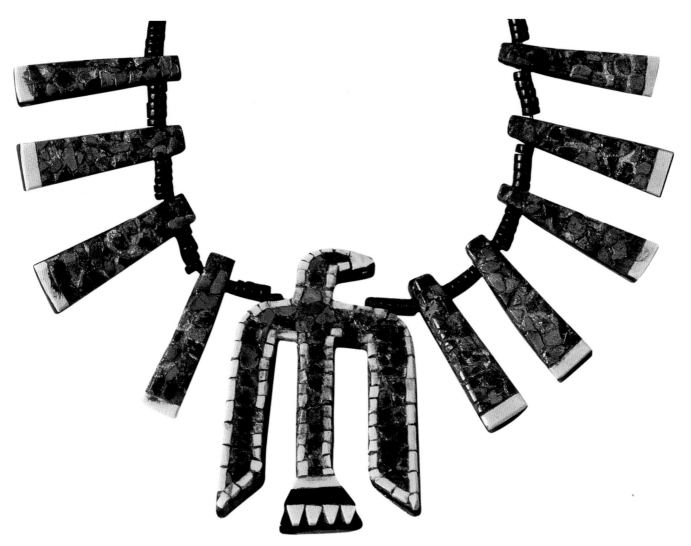

5.3. Santo Domingo thunderbird pendant, crushed stones on Bakelite plastic, 1930s. *Courtesy of Marianne and Bob Kapoun.*

5.4. Fifteen row cuff bracelet set with Blue Gem turquoise; coin silver and square stone settings, probably a Navajo and Zuni collaboration, 1930s. *Courtesy of Lynn D. Trusdell, Crown & Eagle Antiques, Inc.*

5.5. Copper cuff bracelet set with central wrought and embossed silver ornament and small green stone, 1930s. *Courtesy of Lynn D. Trusdell, Crown & Eagle Antiques, Inc.*

5.6. Large cluster bracelet set with Lone Mountain turquoise, ca. 1920s–1930s. *Courtesy of Lynn D. Trusdell, Crown & Eagle Antiques, Inc.*

This decade saw a surge in the development of "cluster work" jewelry (**5.6**, **5.16**, **5.21**): basic jewelry forms, such as naja pendant necklaces, bracelet cuffs, and dangling earrings, were increasingly overlaid with an elaborate multitude of stone settings—in rows, circles, or concentric bands, and in some cases, arranged into broad, asymmetrical patterns. A major reason for the development of cluster work jewelry was the gradual availability of improved tools and equipment that permitted the effective cutting and polishing of nugget-shaped or smooth cabochon turquoise.

Smiths added fine round wire coiled into spiral shapes for decoration, and they augmented these shapes with tiny raindrops created from commercial bead wire. Rounder, button-style earrings appeared in the late 1930s. There were new versions of bracelet forms and concha plaques; conchas became smaller in size and greater in number, so that the seven or eight conchas normally found on belts before 1900 were now replaced by as many as twelve to twenty. Unusual motifs, like the fleur-de-lis, also became popular at this time; while it was an imported design, the fleur-de-lis did resemble imagery found on older Pueblo pottery. Metalware and flatware pieces, a specific type of curio or novelty goods, became popular products in this decade (**5.9**, **5.12**).

Even current events could affect designs: by the late 1930s, Indian traders and native jewelers discontinued the creation and sale of items bearing the swastika, as disapproval of Nazi Germany grew. This development, along with modifications in styles, materials, and forms, were clearly accommodations to the non-Indian market.

Examples of Zuni and other Pueblo mosaic inlay jewelry increased during this decade. Early experiments with this technique were based on the ancient use of mosaic stones on shell; Santo Domingo jewelers used mosaic work on large whole shells, meant as dance shells. Such mosaic inlay could also be set onto silver mounts and on temporary backings made from aluminum. Zuni lapidary skills, in particular, sharpened with expanded explorations of more intricate designs, and this type of mosaic work was taken up by some other Pueblo jewelry-makers and (later on) by Navajo lapidarists. The Pueblos favored certain kinds of motifs for inlay: human figures, birds, and insects, particularly butterflies and dragonflies with outstretched wings. Representations of specific native religious imagery was frowned upon among most Pueblos, but some ceremonially significant figures were conventionalized and used for decorative purposes, probably knowingly so, because of non-Indian interest. For example, at Zuni, a small group of supernatural beings became popular design choices, such as the Knifewing and Rainbow Man (**5.8, 5.9, 5.37**). Some of these figures had their appearances deliberately altered to avoid offending traditionalists' spiritual sensitivities. A number of non-native observers would categorize these inlay pieces as "kachina style," a mode that blossomed more fully in the 1940s and 1950s.

5.7. Zuni inlay choker of the 1930s, possibly by Teddy Weahkee; originally from the C.G. Wallace Collection. *Courtesy of Lynn D. Trusdell, Crown & Eagle Antiques, Inc.*

5.8. Knifewing figure brooch by Dan Simplicio, Zuni, and small turquoise ring, late 1920s or early 1930s. *Courtesy of Lynn D. Trusdell, Crown & Eagle Antiques, Inc.*

5.9. Silver box with turquoise water serpent design on top, 1930s; box may be Navajo and inlay design added by a Zuni. *Courtesy of Lynn D. Trusdell, Crown & Eagle Antiques, Inc.*

Opposite page:
5.10. Delicate multi-strand necklace of hand carved fetish birds, anchored by larger bird with outstretched wings; materials include jet, coral, spiny oyster shell and abalone, Santo Domingo, 1930s. *Courtesy of Lynn D. Trusdell, Crown & Eagle Antiques, Inc.*

The Museum of Northern Arizona now began the first of several important ventures that would aid Southwestern Indian jewelry-making.[1] The museum initiated a Hopi Craftsman Exhibition in 1930 in which two hundred items were displayed and sales neared $1,000 (the exhibition soon became a regular event, and a version of this show continues to the present day). A Navajo Craftsman Exhibition, also sponsored by the museum, was held in June 1936 at Wupatki National Monument.

In addition, museum director Harold Colton and his curator wife, Mary-Russell Ferrell Colton, took a special interest in developing Hopi silverwork as a means of providing some much-needed economic relief to the Hopi communities. In 1938, when there were only twelve Hopi smiths resident on the reservation (compared to ninety at Zuni), the museum launched the Hopi Silver Project: this was meant to encourage a tribally distinctive silverwork technique and style, with some designs drawn from traditional Hopi weaving and pottery, and other motifs drawn from earlier indigenous cultures, such as the Mimbres. Up to that time, Hopi silver jewelry had closely resembled other contemporary Navajo and Pueblo work (**5.36**). The Coltons hoped this planned innovation would bring new attention to Hopi jewelry and produce some badly needed sales. The result of this project became known as "Hopi overlay," a technique that uses two pieces of silver which are soldered onto each other. The top layer has a cut-out design, and the area within that design (where the lower piece shows through) is oxidized to darken it for contrast against the silver top layer. (The overlay technique and style was later popularized by Hopi artist Fred Kabotie and silversmith Paul Saufkie, through a federally assisted training program that was implemented after World War II.)

5.11. Three Zuni-made rings with designs popular in the 1930s; largest ring of jet, spiny oyster shell, and turquoise by Leekya Deyuse. *Courtesy of Lynn D. Trusdell, Crown & Eagle Antiques, Inc.*

5.12. Four examples of silver boxes, mostly Navajo, and set with inlay designs that may be Zuni. Forms include round, card case, cigarette case, and more common square shape, 1930s–1940s. *Courtesy of Lynn D. Trusdell, Crown & Eagle Antiques, Inc.*

5.13. Three sets of early Zuni inlay dangle earrings: top left, turquoise pair by Della Casa Appa, ca. 1925–1935; top right, hoop earrings have open-back bezels characteristic of 1920s; bottom left flat inlay by Dishta, 1940s; bottom right, shell and turquoise work of the late 1930s and early 1940s. *Courtesy of Robert Bauver.*

5.14. This bracelet has appeared in a number of catalogs as Navajo, but is actually the signed work of Zuni silversmith Juan Dedios, 1925–1935. *Courtesy of Robert Bauver.*

5.15. Three bracelets cast from carved tufa molds: one piece has cast in raindrops and others show appliqué add-ons, Navajo or Zuni, 1930s. *Courtesy of Robert Bauver.*

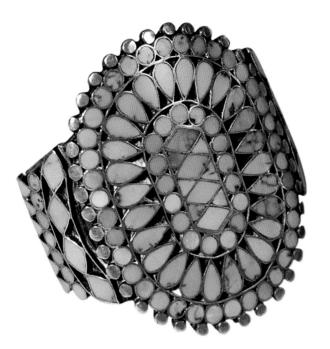
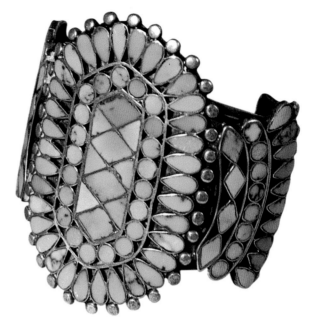

5.16. Two large inlay versions of classic Zuni cluster bracelets by Frank Dishta, late 1930s to early 1940s. *Courtesy of Robert Bauver.*

5.17. Pueblo naja on triple-strand beads, possibly from Cochiti Pueblo. Four stones on the naja, and the round and trefoil beads are small and delicate, ca. 1930s. *Courtesy of Robert Bauver.*

5.18. A "classic" Navajo chisel- and filework silver hatband, ca. 1930s. *Courtesy of Robert Bauver.*

5.19. Commercial tourist thunderbird pendant of lacquered copper, possibly Pueblo, ca. 1930s. *Courtesy of Steven and Mary Delzio.*

5.20. Zuni turquoise ring of early channel work, late 1920s or early 1930s. *Courtesy of Steven and Mary Delzio.*

5.23. Three turquoise and silver row bracelets, two with rounded stone settings and the third with square-stone setting, ca. 1920s–1930s. *Courtesy of Steven and Mary Delzio.*

5.21. Cluster work silver and turquoise bracelet, with twisted wire and two stones on the terminals, ca. 1940, and a ring from the 1930s; both probably Navajo. *Courtesy of Steven and Mary Delzio.*

5.22. Navajo concha belt made from coin silver with six plaques and six butterfly spacers, late 1920s to early 1930s; the buckle may be older. *Courtesy of Steven and Mary Delzio.*

5.24. Three tourist-era bracelets in a variety of popular styles from 1920s and 1930s. *Courtesy of Steven and Mary Delzio.*

5.25. Classic Navajo squash blossom necklace with seven stones on either side, 1930s. *Courtesy of Steven and Mary Delzio.*

5.26. Necklace of hand cut and polished turquoise discs, slightly graduated in size, Pueblo, late 1930s to early 1940s. *Courtesy of Steven and Mary Delzio.*

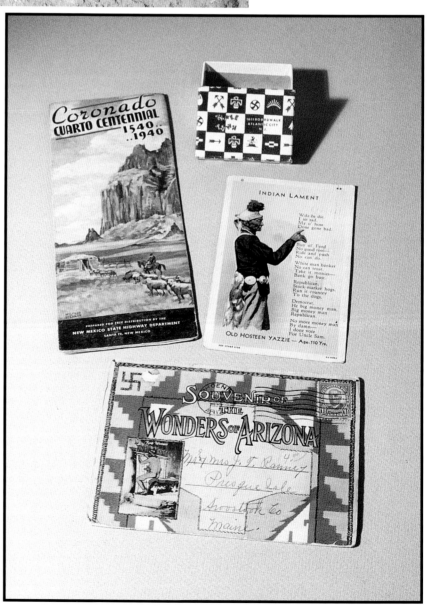

5.27. Tourist brochures from the 1930s and 1940s; including post card of "Indian Lament" and small cardboard jewelry box from a store of the time (in Atlantic City, NJ). *Courtesy of Steven and Mary Delzio.*

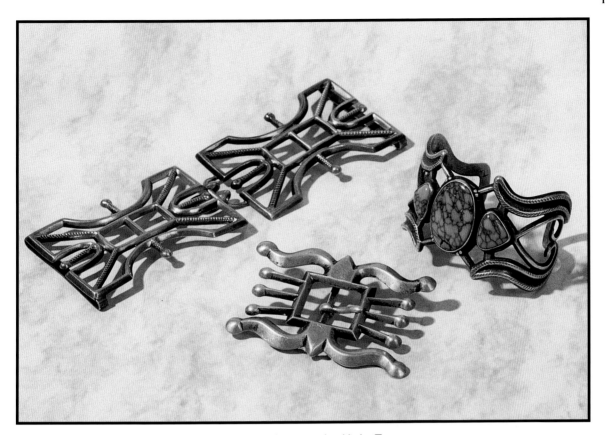

5.28. Navajo buckles by known makers; on lower right, a cast buckle by Tom Burnsides, 1930s or 1940s; on left and upper right, cast buckles by Charlie Houck, also 1930s or 1940s, and a cast bracelet, ca. 1930–1940. *Courtesy of Jay Evetts.*

5.29. Navajo curio or novelty items: top, hair comb from 1930s; on bottom, a Knifewing pill box by Charlie Bitsui, ca. 1940. *Courtesy of Jay Evetts.*

5.30. Five Navajo buttons with turquoise stones, 1920s–1940s; second and third from top bought from a Navajo woman at Chinle, Arizona. *Courtesy of Jay Evetts.*

5.31. Three silver rings set with glass for stones, ca. 1920s–1930s. *Courtesy of Marianne and Bob Kapoun.*

5.32. Three sets of Santo Domingo earrings, ca. 1930s–1940s: earliest are tabs with battery casing backing; smaller birds are backed with older, thicker phonograph record; large birds backed with thinner LP plastic. *Courtesy of Marianne and Bob Kapoun.*

5.33. Group of children's bracelets of thin silver and turquoise, Navajo, 1930s; these are pieces meant for tourist consumption as well as native wear. *Courtesy of Micky and Dolly VanderWagen.*

5.34. A set of bracelet, pendant, and ring in silver and petrified wood, Navajo, from 1930s or 1940s. *Courtesy of Micky and Dolly VanderWagen.*

5.35. Massive silver bracelet set with Santa Rita turquoise, by Roger
Skeet, Navajo, 1930s. *Courtesy of Micky and Dolly VanderWagen.*

5.36. Two Hopi pendants of silver cut outs, filled with Zuni
inlay, 1930s. *Courtesy of Micky and Dolly VanderWagen.*

Other forces did not stay idle during this decade. A number of Southwestern traders banded together in 1931 to form UITA. This new organization was dedicated to boosting mercantile and marketing initiatives and to combat the encroachments of mass-manufactured Indian style goods. The traders' concerns were matched by the U.S. government. On August 27, 1935, the Indian Arts and Crafts Board (IACB), was created—in the fostering spirit of other federal programs started during the New Deal era—to provide oversight of, and protection for, authentic native arts; IACB was authorized to promote exhibitions, marketing, and related endeavors.[2] The board gave grants to the Navajo and Zuni for the eventual creation of guilds, or arts cooperatives. One regulation, signed into effect on March 9, 1937, by Secretary of the Interior John Collier, allowed IACB to establish official stamps that would guarantee an item was genuine and handmade by an Indian. Between 1938 and 1942, stamps marked "U.S. Hopi," "U.S. Navajo," and "U.S. Zuni" were available to participating smiths for use on silver jewelry; this program did not last much past the start of World War II.

One of the most consequential activities of the 1930s was the field work done by the young anthropologist John Adair. In 1937 and 1938, combined with a study of jewelry in major museum collections, Adair interviewed native informants with memories going back to the first decades of smithing. The result, *The Navajo and Pueblo Silversmiths*, was published by the University of Oklahoma Press in 1944, and has been reprinted many times since. Adair's book opens a window onto jewelry-making in the late 1930s. He surveyed techniques in use, preferred designs, and the relationship of silversmithing to native culture. Adair described contemporary practices on the Navajo reservation (with his observations centered around Pine Springs, Arizona) and those at Zuni Pueblo. His appendices contain invaluable dates for the transmission of silversmith activity through the region. The lists of Navajo and Zuni silversmiths active in 1940 has proven to be historically significant documentation. The book vividly treats the kinds of jewelry being made at this time; plain silver pieces, silver bead strings, squash blossom and cross necklaces, and a variety of buttons, pins, and rings are illustrated. Photographs show the range of tools and equipment being used: a homemade blowtorch, old bellows, a drawplate, a railroad tie anvil, and details from the various steps involved in casting from a mold.

Non-native attitudes about Indian jewelry were taking various forms throughout the 1930s. Many people still viewed this decoration as "primitive" and made by "savage smiths." Such phrases were used in an article in the March 1934 issue of *Design*, which went on to claim that the native "art of silversmithing degenerated and died out" by this decade.[3] The article also mirrored the feelings of serious collectors of older silverwork—namely, that later works were lacking in quality. Already there was a split in popular sentiment about preferred types of Southwestern Indian jewelry. While the market for older jewelry was now being defined, those promoting contemporary native jewelry sought to make distinctions between these older pieces (which possessed a look often portrayed as classical, using a fixed set of design elements) and new work. Plus many traders, dealers, and even some museum curators, wanted to see jewelry that looked unique to a specific native group. This led to the promulgation of interest in "tribal styles," a short-lived direction for new native jewelry design that would dissipate with the rise of pan-Indianism (a cooperative movement among native peoples meant to boost pride in their common heritage) in the 1960s. One successful example of a deliberate creation of a tribal style can be seen in Hopi overlay. Pieces could also be seen as made in the "Zuni style," emphasizing multiple stonework, or "Navajo style," featuring silver with strong die stamping.

Throughout the 1930s, intensified marketing activities—such as the creation of the New Mexico Tourist Bureau in 1935—were instituted to counter the effects of the Depression. By 1936, the annual sales show held in Santa Fe had become an "Indian Market"; the market's sponsor, the New Mexico Association on Indian Affairs, a political advocacy group, was beginning its slow transformation into the organization known today as SWAIA (Southwestern Association for Indian Arts). And the occasional retail campaign appeared: in 1934, for example, R. H. Macy & Co. in New York City promoted Southwestern Indian products, including a collection of silver jewelry.

In 1939, the promotion of Southwestern native jewelry received a boost at the Golden Gate International Exposition in San Francisco, which brought 1 1/4 million visitors to view large displays of Southwestern Indian arts, including Navajo silverwork. The show's popularity led IACB to sponsor another exhibition the following year, one that would prove to be of equal, if not greater, aid to the promotion of Indian jewelry (see chapter 6).

5.37. Silver cuff bracelet with Knifewing inlay design of coral and white shell; silver by Charlie Bitsui, Navajo, and inlay by Lambert Homer Sr., Zuni, ca. 1935. *Courtesy of Micky and Dolly VanderWagen.*

5.38. Two inlay brooches of Pueblo women, Zuni, possibly by Leo Poblano, 1930s. *Courtesy of Micky and Dolly VanderWagen.*

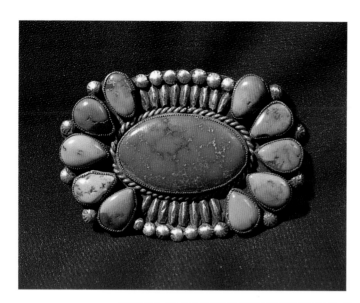

5.39. Silver brooch with early green and blue turquoise cluster pattern, Zuni, late 1930s. *Courtesy of Micky and Dolly VanderWagen.*

5.40. Two hand-wrought silver bracelets with petrified wood settings, Navajo, 1930s. *Courtesy of Micky and Dolly VanderWagen.*

5.41. Navajo-made beads from scrap silver, hammered and rolled, 1930s or 1940s; these were cheaper materials to purchase, but more difficult to work. *Courtesy of Micky and Dolly VanderWagen.*

5.42. Navajo-made concha belt with early use of imitation turquoise used for cluster effect on conchas and belt buckle, early 1930s. *Private collection.*

5.43. Concha belt with seven concha plaques and seven spacers on black leather by Austin Wilson, Navajo, 1930s; bright turquoise stones for central detail. *Private collection.*

5.44. Three pairs of Zuni earrings (all are from former collection of C.G. Wallace); left; attributed to Della Casa Appa; middle: John Gordon Leak; right: Frank Vacit, 1930s to 1940s. *Courtesy of Carol and John Krena.*

5.45. Finely designed Blue Gem turquoise channel work bracelet cuff with silver stamping, 1930s. *Courtesy of Carol and John Krena.*

5.46. Zuni-made inlay rings with coral, shell, jet, and turquoise; large size meant they were made for sale to Utes in the 1930s. *Courtesy of Micky and Dolly VanderWagen.*

By the 1930s, an individual silversmith's work might sometimes receive public attention. Some artists were influential because they taught in the region's Indian schools. During this decade, Fred Peshlakai instructed the next generation's leading Navajo smith, Kenneth Begay, at the Fort Wingate Boarding School. Zuni jeweler Ted Weahkee taught silversmithing to students at the Santa Fe Indian School. John Adair profiled the abilities of Navajo jewelry-makers Tom Burnsides, Charlie Houck, Ambrose Roanhorse, and John Six. At Zuni, Lanyade was still alive in 1937, when Adair interviewed him to learn the early history of silversmithing at the pueblo. Keneshde, one of the first smiths to place turquoise on silver, was also interviewed. Younger Zuni smiths and their work received attention, including Horace Iule (Adair spells it "Aiule"), Raymond and Jerry Watson, and Okweene Neese. The designs of Weahkee and two other Zuni lapidarists, Leekya Deyuse and Juan Dedios, were also praised at this time. Rio Grande jewelers were lesser known, probably because of their smaller numbers: San Ildefonso only acquired its own silversmith in 1930. For the most part, however, jewelry-makers remained anonymous craftsmen to the majority of non-native consumers during this decade.

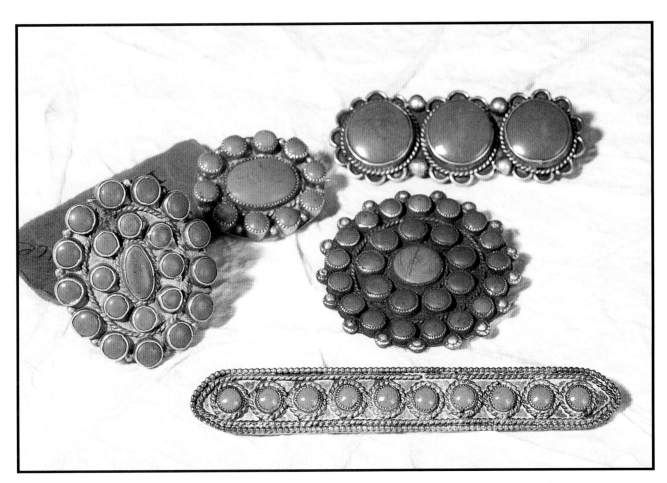

5.47. Imitation turquoise in use on a variety of jewelry forms, 1930s. *Courtesy of Micky and Dolly VanderWagen.*

5.48. Two Zuni dragonfly pins; left: in turquoise nugget style, by Leo Poblano, 1930s (formerly in the collection of Leo Coriz "Pancho"); right: inlay circle pin, by John Gordon Leak, ca. 1930s (formerly in the collection of C.G. Wallace). An unusual feature is Leak's use of coral rather than spiny oyster shell in the piece. *Courtesy of Carol and John Krena.*

[1]Margaret Nickelson Wright, *Hopi Silver: The History and Hallmarks of Hopi Silversmithing*, rev. and expanded ed. (Flagstaff: Northland, 1989), pp. 37-47.

[2]See Robert F. Schrader, *The Indian Arts and Crafts Board: An Aspect of New Deal Policy* (Albuquerque: University of New Mexico, 1983).

[3]Emily Farnham, "Decorative Design in Indian Jewelry," *Design* 35 (March 1934): 15.

Chapter 6.
The 1940s:
The Effects of War and Peace

Many Navajo and Pueblo men served in the armed forces during World War II; more than two hundred enlisted from Zuni Pueblo alone. One group, a special corps of Navajo Marines based in the South Pacific and known as the Code Talkers, utilized a form of encrypted messages derived from their own language that the Japanese were never able to decipher. The disruptions of war naturally affected native jewelry-making. For example, during the war years, the U.S. War Production Board sought to cut the silver supply for nonmilitary use. Indian arts advocates, including the Indian Arts and Crafts Board (IACB), traders, and museum professionals (such as the Coltons), argued that native smiths needed continuing access to silver for pressing economic reasons. Even with this support, silver became difficult to obtain by late 1942, and it remained scarce until the war's end.

Even without the impact of Native American participants in the war, a new world was dawning in which native individuals, rather than anonymous groups, were gaining credibility. At the start of the decade, however, this was still difficult to see: the *Gallup Independent* of August 17, 1940, while reporting on the arts exhibited at the annual Gallup Inter-tribal Ceremonial stated "...Individual Indians showed greater interest in this feature of the Ceremonial than heretofore but many of their exhibits were entered under the displays of various traders." Still actively engaged in promoting cooperative marketing outlets for native work, the IACB aided in the start-up of the Navajo Arts and Crafts Enterprise (later Guild) in 1941, and silversmith Ambrose Roanhorse was appointed its first director (**6.1, 6.2**).

6.2. Detail of hallmark on buckle. *Courtesy of Robert Bauver.*

6.1. Smaller-sized concha belt with eleven plaques and buckle showing hallmark of the Navajo Arts and Crafts Guild, 1940s–1950s. *Courtesy of Robert Bauver.*

6.3. Twisted wire and turquoise pin attributed to Fred Peshlakai, Navajo, 1940s. *Courtesy of Carol and John Krena.*

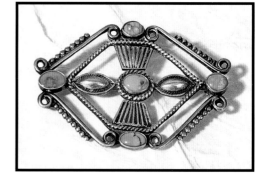

Prior to the U.S. entry into the war, backing from the IACB had led to an exhibition that gave Southwestern Indian jewelry greater prominence: this was "Indian Art of the United States," which ran from January 22 to April 27, 1941, at the Museum of Modern Art in New York City. This exhibition brought new attention to Southwestern Indian jewelry at a time when all forms of "Americana" were being boosted. IACB keenly exploited New York's status as an influential center for art and fashion trends. The organization made arrangements to have Indian jewelry sold in the city's major department stores, advertised in major newspapers, and mentioned in such publications as *Woman's Wear Daily* as part of a strategically targeted publicity and retail sales campaign. Two Navajo smiths, Dooley Shorty (who appears in the museum's records as Shorty Dooley) and Tom Katenay, were brought in to demonstrate silversmithing during the exhibition.[1] (After the Japanese attack on Pearl Harbor, Shorty enlisted in the Marines, and he became one of the first Navajo Code Talkers.)

Those who attended the exhibition "Indian Art of the United States" were shown a distinctive range of silverwork; many of the pieces on display formed a concrete repertoire of now familiar styles and techniques. Items depicted in the exhibition catalogue include a squash blossom necklace with twelve trefoil beads and a double-barred naja pendant, a sandcast bracelet and pin, a concha belt, a *ketoh,* and a twisted wire bracelet with square-cut turquoise. Zuni inlay pins featuring the Knifewing, Rainbow Man, and a mask of the Shalako figure Saiyatasha were also featured in the catalogue (**6.5, 6.6, 6.7, 6.8**). Frederic Douglas and Rene D'Harnoncourt, the exhibition's organizers, offered decisive statements about the relevance of these pieces: "The most striking evidence of the affinity between traditional Indian art and modern art forms can be seen in Navaho [*sic*] silver."[2]

6.4. Concha belt with six large silver conchas and decorative buckle by Roger Skeet, Navajo, and Rainbow deity inlaid on silver by Rose Pincio, Zuni, 1940s. *Private collection.*

6.5. Knifewing inlay figure on bracelet, Zuni, 1940s. *Author's collection.*

6.6. Zuni inlay earrings by Dan Simplicio, depicting Knifewing figures, 1930s or 1940s. *Courtesy of Lynn D. Trusdell, Crown & Eagle Antiques, Inc.*

6.7. Sophisticated mid-twentieth-century Zuni inlay jewelry; masks on extreme left and right with raised inlay details by Leo Poblano show influence of his first wife, sculptress Daisy Hooee Nampeyo; a small Knifewing figure in center, also by Leo Poblano; below, a center-inlaid shell figure, by Teddy Weahkee, shaped as a piece of pottery. Earrings have been attributed to Leekya Deyuse by C.G. Wallace. *Courtesy of Robert Bauver.*

6.8. Seven mosaic inlay Zuni pins from the former C.G. Wallace Collection, 1940s. *Courtesy of Lynn D. Trusdell, Crown & Eagle Antiques, Inc.*

Ambrose Roanhorse attended the exhibition's opening, where he spoke with Eleanor Roosevelt about contemporary silverwork instruction at the Indian schools; the first lady was clearly impressed with what she heard, and her approval of Indian school training made its way into her "My Day" newspaper column on January 27, 1941. Production increased as a result of this interest, and Sophie Aberle, the superintendent of the United Pueblos Agency, reported in the March 7, 1941, issue of the *Phoenix Gazette* that, "The Navajos are now having difficulty supplying the demand for silver designs."

Even during the war years, native jewelers and smiths continued to utilize changes in materials and techniques to their advantage. In a 1943 article entitled "Silversmithing Survives," David Neumann, an Indian arts expert, noted the Indian jewelry-maker's ". . . willingness to adapt his skill to the continually changing requirements of the market and to his changing way of life."[3] Neumann expressed concern about the lack of silver for smiths in 1943, and that they might be forced to return to using coin silver. Certainly, early forms of plastic first made their way into jewelry inlay during the 1940s (and plastic continues to be used today). Many copper jewelry pieces were contributed for recycling as part of the war's need for metals (**6.9, 6.10, 6.11**), and many examples of these pieces disappeared forever.

6.9. Copper Indian style tourist bracelet, 1940s. *Author's collection.*

6.10. Copper tourist metalwork pieces designed and made by Tom Weahkee, Zuni. Some pieces set with Morenci turquoise, and some show on back the hallmark Weahkee devised after teaching at the Santa Fe Indian School, 1930s and 1940s. *Courtesy of Micky and Dolly VanderWagen.*

6.11. Copper tourist jewelry made by Tom Weahkee, Zuni, 1930s and 1940s, including an unusual cast copper buckle. *Courtesy of Micky and Dolly VanderWagen.*

The war's end brought new developments. Native artisans increasingly made their pieces with commercial findings, such as pins and screw-backs (**6.21**). Traders ordered postwar acetylene blowtorches, power drills, and dies and distributed them to smiths working in areas that were now receiving electricity. By the late 1940s, lapidarists were enjoying the use of such power tools as cutters, grinders, and buffing wheels. These conveniences altered jewelry-making techniques in other ways; for example, channel work could now be created with larger silver bands between the stone settings (**6.15**). A bent-wire method introduced in 1949 made channels easier to construct and hold in place. However, it should also be noted that as jewelry fabrication moved further away from the fully hand-wrought, many Indian arts advocates showed strong signs of disapproval.

In keeping with the sense of growing change that pervaded the 1940s, jewelry forms and designs now showed greater evidence of external influence. Indian jewelry was promoted widely as costume jewelry, and pieces were made that adhered more closely to mainstream styles. For example, the decade saw the introduction of native-made watchbands and watch bracelets, barrettes, tie tacs, and the bola tie (**6.23**, **6.24**). The popularity of squash blossom necklaces decreased in favor of shorter necklaces; in fact, Hopi jewelry-makers largely abandoned the squash blossom style for shorter-length pendant necklaces or chokers by the late 1940s (**6.14**, **6.22**). Zuni stonework styles continued to evolve. Better tools for cutting and shaping led to the creation of techniques using small stone shaping: the needlepoint style—with elongated narrow stones pointed at the ends—appeared between 1946 and 1948, closely followed by the petitpoint (elongated stones with rounded ends) and nugget styles (**6.30**). It is significant to note that writers at this time suddenly attributed the creation of the nugget style to one individual, Dan Simplicio. Floral and leaf motifs were popular; outstanding examples of such designs could be seen in the work of young Navajo smiths Kenneth Begay and his cousin Allan Kee, working at the White Hogan shop in Arizona.

Hopi jewelry—especially the new Hopi overlay style—received a boost after the war. A training program on silversmithing, funded by the G.I. Bill, was started in February 1947. Lasting eighteen months, the course paid fifteen Hopi veterans for training, tools, and living expenses. Fred Kabotie and Paul Saufkie taught this program in New Oraibi (first at Hopi High School, and later in a nearby Quonset hut). The students often used copper for practice work, but their experiments with using sheet silver in a variety of thicknesses, matting of oxidized surfaces, and cut-out designs added new dimensions to overlay work. Further refinements included added textures and repoussé effects (**6.12**, **6.13**, **6.14**). The first class of this program graduated in 1949, and a second class finished in 1951. Overlay was on display at the 1949 Hopi Craftsman Exhibit at the Museum of Northern Arizona. The Hopi Silvercraft Guild was also started in 1949. By the end of the 1940s, a remarkable range of silver Hopi overlay jewelry had been created by such pioneer designers as Fred Kabotie, Herbert Komayouse, Pierce Kewanwytewa, Clarence Lomayestewa, Bert Puhuyestewa, Paul Saufkie, and Orville Talayumptewa.

6.12. Overlay design silver bolo slide with elongated metal tips, Hopi, ca. late 1940s. *Courtesy of Steven and Mary Delzio.*

6.13. Hopi overlay ring with unusually large turquoise setting, late 1940s–1950s. *Author's collection.*

6.14. Hopi silver necklace in the overlay style, featuring a small squirrel or other rodent, late 1940s or 1950s. *Courtesy of Micky and Dolly VanderWagen.*

6.15. Pair of channel inlay bracelet cuffs by Bernard Homer Sr., Zuni, 1940s. *Courtesy of Micky and Dolly VanderWagen.*

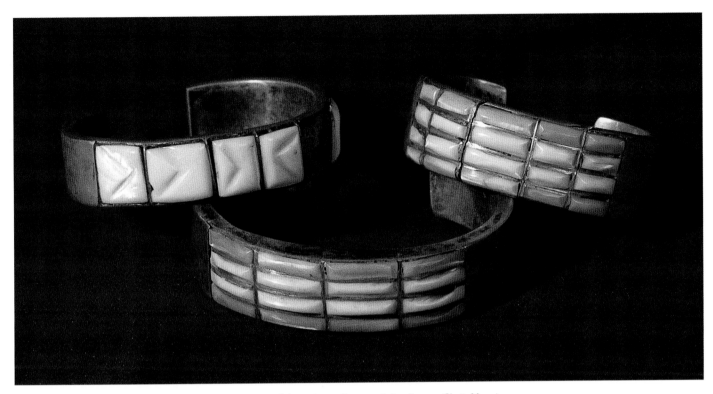

6.16. Three white shell inlay bracelets, made as a collaboration: silver work by James Chai, Navajo, and inlay by Juanita Homer, Zuni, ca. 1945. *Courtesy of Micky and Dolly VanderWagen.*

6.17. Three-strand fetish carved necklace by Leekya Deyuse; features animals and birds, with a variety of stones, late 1940s. *Courtesy of Micky and Dolly VanderWagen.*

6.18. Detail of central pendant animal on Leekya necklace. *Courtesy of Micky and Dolly VanderWagen.*

6.19. Silver bead choker, made by Tom Yazzie, Navajo, with carved turquoise birds by Leekya Deyuse, and matching earrings, late 1940s. *Courtesy of Micky and Dolly VanderWagen.*

6.20. A Zuni inlay of a bulls' head on deer vertebrae, 1940s. *Courtesy of Micky and Dolly VanderWagen.*

6.21. A pair of Blue Gem turquoise channel earrings, with raised channel work in the center, originally screwbacks, late 1940s–1950s. *Courtesy of Robert Bauver.*

6.22. Turquoise and silver choker with leaf pattern made from petitpoint stones, and surrounded by silver raindrops, Zuni, ca. 1940s or 1950s. *Courtesy of Steven and Mary Delzio.*

6.23. Three Zuni bolos from the 1940s: at left is Knifewing on white shell, center has Pueblo sun face or sun shield design, and on right, a Shalako figure by Leo Poblano. *Courtesy of Robert Bauver.*

6.24. Early channel work man's watch bracelet of blue-green turquoise with silver leaves supporting working watch face, Zuni, 1940s. *Courtesy of Steven and Mary Delzio.*

6.25. Three inlay Zuni bracelets: bottom center cluster piece is Blue Gem turquoise from 1940s. Above are two heavy silver cuffs: left is turquoise and shell work collaboration by Lambert Homer Sr., Zuni, and Roger Skeet, Navajo, 1940s, originally from collection of trader C.G. Wallace; right, multi-stone inlay design from late 1940s or early 1950s. *Courtesy of Robert Bauver.*

6.26. Channel work turquoise and silver choker of Zuni make, 1940s.
Courtesy of Lynn D. Trusdell, Crown & Eagle Antiques, Inc.

6.27. Zuni silver paperweight owned originally by trader C.G. Wallace, with turquoise channel inlay of the Knifewing deity, ca. 1940s. Also a collaboration piece by Roger Skeet, Navajo, and Lambert Homer Sr., Zuni. *Courtesy of Robert Bauver.*

6.28. Two unusual pieces: on left, a coral cast bracelet signed by Mary Marie, Navajo, and on the right, a Zuni manta pin made into a bracelet, 1940s–1950s. *Courtesy of Robert Bauver.*

6.29. An early inlay ring by Frank Vacit, Zuni, from the former C.G. Wallace collection, 1940s. *Courtesy of Robert Bauver.*

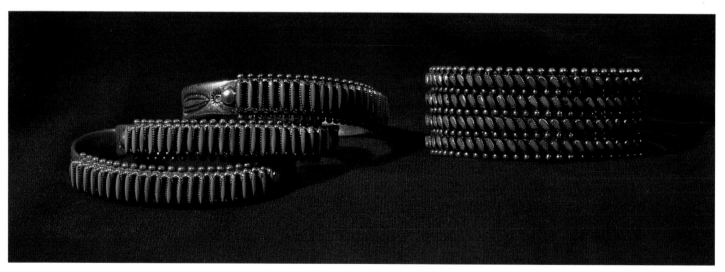

6.30. A unique Zuni lapidary style: one petitpoint and three needlepoint turquoise on silver bracelets, 1940s. *Courtesy of Micky and Dolly VanderWagen.*

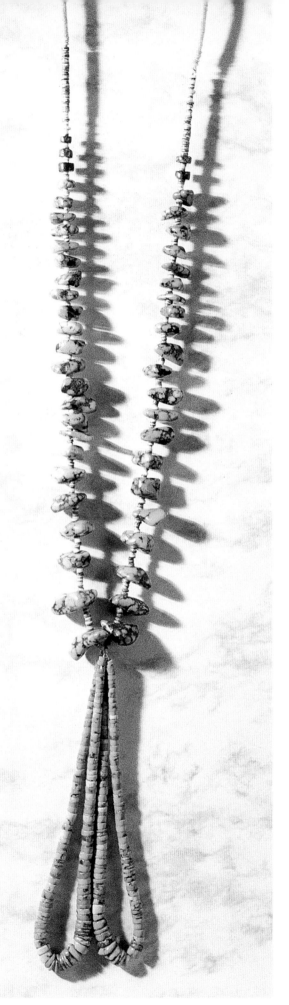

6.31. Single strand turquoise necklace with double jaclas tied on, late 1940s to early 1950s. *Courtesy of Steven and Mary Delzio.*

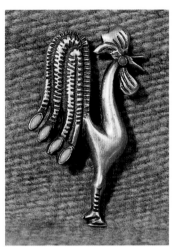

6.32. Tourist silver pin of rooster set with glass, possibly Pueblo-made, and probably 1940s. *Courtesy of Marianne and Bob Kapoun.*

6.33. Thunderbird pendant on Bakelite plastic by Clara Reano, Santo Domingo, probably 1940s. *Courtesy of Marianne and Bob Kapoun.*

6.34. Large turquoise pin pendant, Zuni, attributed to Dan Simplicio, 1940s. *Courtesy of Lynn D. Trusdell, Crown & Eagle Antiques, Inc.*

Below:
6.36. Large cluster bracelet of Lone Mountain turquoise by Warren Ondelacy, Zuni, late 1940s. *Courtesy of Micky and Dolly VanderWagen.*

6.35. Gold and silver thunderbird pin, probably 1940s. *Private collection.*

6.40. Five rings made from silver and set with petrified wood, 1940s and 1950s. *Courtesy of Lynn D. Trusdell, Crown & Eagle Antiques, Inc.*

6.37. Three pieces by noted Zuni master carver Leekya Deyuse: bear fetish figure; turquoise frog on silver box; frog ring, 1930s–1940s. *Courtesy of Lynn D. Trusdell, Crown & Eagle Antiques, Inc.*

6.38. Silver "blanks" or forms: row bracelet by unknown maker, and antelope pin by Sam Bahe, Navajo, 1940s. *Courtesy of Micky and Dolly VanderWagen.*

6.39. Five rings featuring large chunk or nugget turquoise stones, Zuni, 1930s–1940s. *Courtesy of Micky and Dolly VanderWagen.*

6.41. Kachina-style silver tourist pin by Alfonso Roybal, 1940s. *Author's collection.*

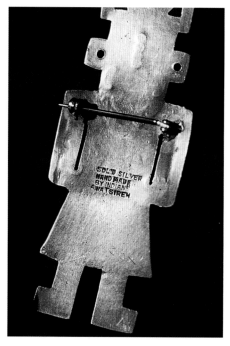

6.42. Back of pin with unusual signature stamp. *Author's collection.*

Other postwar developments increased new options for jewelry creation. The United Indian Traders Association increased their promotion of Indian jewelry after 1945. In addition, cash payments were rapidly replacing credit at the trading post, resulting in a decline of the pawn system. And an important alternative to the standard payment method—whereby a native jeweler received payment by the piece—took place around 1947 when John and Virginia Bonnell, owners of the White Hogan in Scottsdale, Arizona, began a new compensation plan with their in-house smith, Kenneth Begay. Within a few years, Begay was drawing a regular salary and received a percentage of the shop's profits.[4] Over the next two decades, those silversmiths who worked under such a system received a greater financial incentive to be innovative and experimental in their work. Others produced tourist silver work as a means of receiving steady wages; for example, Pueblo artist Awa Tsireh (Alfonso Roybal; San Ildefonso) worked for the Garden of the Gods Trading Post in Colorado Springs, Colorado, during this decade (**6.41, 6.42**).

The renewed supply of commercially available sheet silver and wire made the hammering of slugs and hand-drawing of wire largely unnecessary. In addition, turquoise mining resumed in Arizona, Colorado, and Nevada. There was also the highly significant postwar introduction of synthetic, or imitation, turquoise—an innovation that would eventually bring major changes to native jewelry-making. Also, the late 1940s brought road improvements around the Navajo reservation, including the highway between Gallup and Zuni.

This decade can be seen as a dividing line between older style jewelry and a growing modernization. While the marketplace dictated changes in jewelry forms and designs meant to appeal more to mainstream American adornment tastes, many Indian arts experts and collectors continued to laud works from earlier decades. Interestingly, the Depression years had created an enlarged group of dedicated collectors of Indian jewelry. Throughout the 1940s, many of these collectors had jobs related to (or other connections with) three Santa Fe institutions—the Santa Fe Indian School, the Indian Arts Fund, and the Laboratory of Anthropology, all of which maintained programs that encouraged native smiths to use the older types of design in their work. Writers in local magazines also praised earlier jewelry styles, and specific recommendations to collectors and consumers begin to appear. One article in the December 1941 issue of *Arizona Highways* strongly condemned the effects of tourism on Navajo silverwork.[5] The article notes collectors' preferences for irregularly cut and polished hand-wrought pieces, and admonishes buyers to choose only older turquoise stones of a light cerulean blue. Other types of jewelry favored by collectors at the time included necklaces with large round beads, and flat, broad band bracelets having diameters of one inch to three and a half inches. Another *Arizona Highways* article from 1944 advised consumers to buy "marked silver" made from good-quality silver slugs. Many contemporary jewelers fashioned fairly elaborate, even baroque, heavy silver pieces throughout the decade in an attempt to capture sales.

An important indicator of bias in favor of older jewelry was the growing use of the term "classical" in relation to pre-1940 work (this was actually an extension of the term, which in the previous decade had been applied to works produced before 1930). This classification was meant to convey a sense of authority, especially in the face of change, and it was part of a nostalgia movement that became evident during this time. Newspapers and magazines that reported on Southwestern Indian silverwork used such descriptions as "classic forms" and "classic adornment" for this jewelry as a whole. Contemporary accounts of the works of Navajos Ambrose Roanhorse and Tom Burnsides, along with descriptions of pieces by Santo Domingo smith Vidal Aragon, praised their "elegant style" and "classical creations." As a consequence, certain types of mainstream adaptations were often mistaken for tourist efforts. This value system would have a powerful effect on the antique Indian jewelry market, and it would lead in time to contemporary artists' explorations and revivals of certain early styles (see Chapter 7).

The 1940s can also be viewed as a separating line between "traditional" jewelry forms and styles, and the variations that would inevitably grow in the years following the war. It did not matter that traditional Southwestern Indian jewelry, as far as metal jewelry was concerned, was less than one hundred years old. By the end of the decade, the types of jewelry featured in the 1941 "Indian Art of the United States" exhibition were already classics in themselves. Navajo and Pueblo silver jewelry had acquired its own tradition.

6.43. Inlay bracelet of mother of pearl and white fresh water clam shell on silver; depicts masks of the Longhorn kachinas, by unknown Zuni maker, ca. 1948. *Courtesy of Micky and Dolly VanderWagen.*

6.44. Detail of Zuni inlay mask on bracelet. *Courtesy of Micky and Dolly VanderWagen.*

6.45. Inlay figure of Hopi maiden by Leo Poblano, Zuni, 1940s. *Courtesy of Carol and John Krena.*

6.46. Two tufa molds used for casting jewelry: on left, a *ketoh* design; and right, a lizard possibly carved by Dan Simplicio, Zuni. *Courtesy of Micky and Dolly VanderWagen.*

* * *

Reactions to the sweeping social changes brought about by global war and its aftermath mark the 1940s. The Indians of New Mexico and Arizona won the right to vote only in 1948. Tourism in the region had slumped during the first half of the decade but then revived during the late 1940s. The decade, however, was a bridge to a new future. Native men had traveled abroad as warriors and returned with new sights and experiences in mind. Many native women worked, as most American women did, for the war effort, even if their work was local and served as a substitution for the arts made by the absent men. While silver and turquoise jewelry would no longer be made as it had been in the late nineteenth and early twentieth centuries, the memory of such work would never be left behind. Soon, postwar native silversmiths and jewelers would make a new kind of jewelry—thoroughly modern, but with tangible links to the past.

[1]Paula A. Baxter, "Navajo and Pueblo Jewelry, 1940-1970: Three Decades of Innovative Design Revisited," *American Indian Art Magazine* 21 (autumn 1996): 36.

[2]Frederic Douglas and Rene D'Harnoncourt, *Indian Art of the United States* (New York: Museum of Modern Art, 1941), p. 201.

[3]David Neumann, "Navajo Silversmithing Survives," *El Palacio* 50, 1 (January 1943): 6.

[4]Arthur Woodward, "Navajo Silver Comes of Age," *Quarterly of the Los Angeles County Museum* 10, 1 (1953): 12.

[5]Catherine Chambliss, "Metal of the Moon," pp. 35-37.

Chapter 7.
The 1950s to mid-1960s:
A Popular Art

The 1950s brought a resolute end to the craft work status of native-made silver and turquoise jewelry. By 1950, Southwestern Indian jewelry could be divided into three distinct categories, with each category playing its own role within the Indian arts market. The first category was composed of *older, or "antique," native-made jewelry*: this included silver pieces made during the first thirty to sixty years of silversmithing, plus items of turquoise or other natural materials that could have been made even earlier. Antique Indian jewelry, often called "old pawn" or "dead pawn," was an exclusive commodity, since even by 1950 much of it was hard to obtain. It was generally more expensive than contemporary jewelry, with the finest pieces possessing the aura of historical artifacts (see Chapter 8 for more discussion of pawn jewelry). The second category, generally labeled as *craft work*, was contemporary native-made jewelry usually created by a combination of hand fabrication and powered tool processes. Such jewelry was sold at trading posts, shops, and Indian arts shows (**7.5**). This type represented the largest category of commodities for sale, and such authentic work was subject to a variety of influences, both native and mainstream non-native in origin; while Indian jewelry continued to be made according

7.1. Three belt buckles from the 1950s and 1960s, in a variety of popular turquoise stone settings. *Courtesy of Micky and Dolly VanderWagen.*

7.2. Blank of a wide cuff bracelet, uncompleted, turquoise oval stone in place, Navajo, 1950s. *Courtesy of Micky and Dolly VanderWagen.*

7.4. Leaf style silver necklace with pyrite and pink coral stones, by Dan Simplicio, Zuni, 1950s. *Courtesy of Micky and Dolly VanderWagen.*

7.3. A blank for a five-row silver bracelet of Navajo make, and a completed piece set with turquoise by Zuni lapidarist Rose Jackson, 1950s. *Courtesy of Micky and Dolly VanderWagen.*

7.5. Pair of large Zuni Rainbow Man bolo tie slides, showing intricate inlay of the late 1950s and the 1960s. *Courtesy of Micky and Dolly VanderWagen.*

to prescribed forms and styles, the non-native demand for costume jewelry pieces was stronger than ever. The final category was *mass-produced Indian jewelry*, including both items that might have been made by Indians in a bench shop setting and others that were devoid of any real connection with Indian creation. While this category was not a clear-cut product of native endeavor itself, it was an established part of the market by the 1950s. Such jewelry was characterized by generic designs, imitated or adapted from authentic work and then conventionalized (often into stereotyped motifs); it was also made from cheaper, lightweight materials. These pieces were bought largely as tourist souvenirs or costume jewelry, and were very inexpensive. And it was this third category—representing the negative side of the Indian arts market—that tarnished the value and image of the authentic commodities represented in the first and second categories, because collectors were exposed to deliberate fakes and forgeries, or reproductions offered through misrepresentation.

7.6. Silver and twisted wire Navajo cuff bracelet, 1950s. *Author's collection.*

7.7. Rolled silver hatband, Navajo, with Last Chance Mine turquoise, 1950s. *Courtesy of Micky and Dolly VanderWagen.*

7.8. Loop earrings with dangles made with turquoise from the Last Chance Mine, late 1940s–1950s; this style was popular with Pueblo women. *Courtesy of Micky and Dolly VanderWagen.*

7.9. Seven rings with inlay kachina figures on hammered silver, Zuni, late 1940s or early 1950s. *Courtesy of Micky and Dolly VanderWagen.*

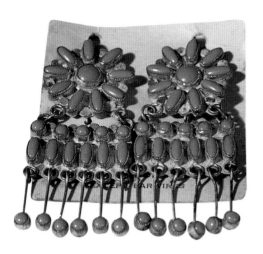

7.10. Fancy cluster and dangle earrings, with imitation turquoise, Zuni, 1950s. *Courtesy of Micky and Dolly VanderWagen.*

With each category of Indian (or imitation Indian) jewelry in some kind of demand, the sheer volume of items produced, by hand or by machine, was greater in the 1950s than at any previous time. Pieces could be made more intricate because the materials and tools required for such work were now more readily available than ever before. More extensive rural electrification brought motor-driven equipment to native lapidarists; by 1950, such labor savers as diamond-tooth saws were in use at Zuni. As a result, cluster work and related techniques, became more prevalent at the pueblo. Native jewelers saw new applications for the use of turquoise and coral stone shavings; one notable example is the chip inlay technique, which began to appear around the early 1960s. Traders and other middlemen encouraged such changes in jewelry styles; some native smiths made styles to suit retail fashion seasons during the 1950s.[1] This development indicates serious attempts by the Indian jewelry industry to boost the viability of these goods as costume or dress jewelry. The growing popularity of Western wear helped to introduce Indian silverwork accessories, such as the fairly new bola tie and ranger belt sets (**7.11, 7.12**). The silver overlay style originated by the Hopis also prospered: by the late 1950s, this technique was taught in virtually all Indian schools' jewelry-making programs. The Hopi smiths increasingly began to finish their pieces by rubbing them with steel wool, thus giving Hopi overlay jewelry a soft finish that made this type of work more distinct from other Southwestern native jewelry (**7.13, 7.14, 7.15**).

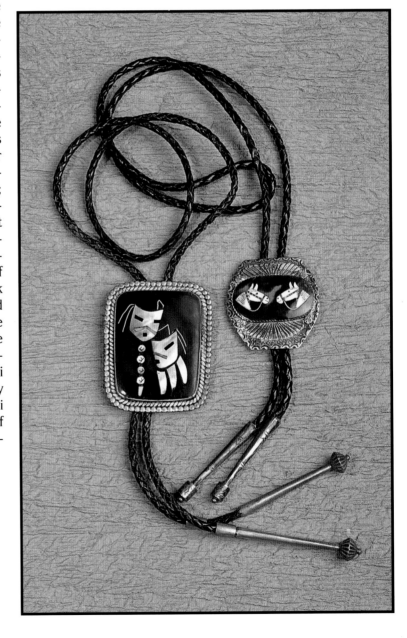

7.11. Two Zuni bolo ties set with tortoise shell, with motifs of masks and horse heads, 1950s. *Courtesy of Lynn D. Trusdell, Crown & Eagle Antiques, Inc.*

7.12. Inlay ranger set with unusual turkey motif, Zuni, 1950s–1960s. *Author's collection.*

7.13. Large double-sided Hopi overlay pendant, showing one side depicting a pottery design, unknown maker, 1950s. *Courtesy of Steven and Mary Delzio.*

7.14. Verso of pendant depicts a water serpent. *Courtesy of Steven and Mary Delzio.*

7.15. Hopi silver overlay bracelet depicting a processional scene, including an antelope dancer among others, stamped inside "S. Tom," late 1950s. *Courtesy of Lynn D. Trusdell, Crown & Eagle Antiques, Inc.*

During the 1950s, individual artists began to receive some recognition on a more regular basis: for example, the *Gallup Independent* of August 8, 1950, showed photos of a Knifewing inlay pin by the recently deceased Alonzo Hustito of Zuni, along with a Rainbow Man by Daisy and Leo Poblano (who were named in the caption as the first artists to design modern inlay figures). Winners of the prizes at the 1950 Gallup Inter-tribal Ceremonial included Kenneth Begay, whose silver cigarette box won the Elkus Award ("for new silver objects that will have commercial value and open a new field for Indian silver handicraft"). Other prize winners named were Charlie Bitsui (Navajo) and Virgil Dishta (Zuni). And by the 1960s, reporting on ceremonial arts exhibits and awards focused on the artists, rather than the traders they worked for. Greater attention was also paid to young silversmiths, both male and female.

Publications that promoted tourism, such as *Arizona Highways* and *New Mexico Magazine*, increasingly featured articles on native arts that included jewelry-making. The influx of tourists, especially along historic Route 66, picked up considerably in the 1950s and 1960s. The urge to produce Indian goods for tourist sales brought developments that made native traditionalists uneasy. For example, a new form of smaller-scale, permanent (and therefore commercialized) Navajo sandpainting was produced for sale to tourists around 1958. The use of kachina figures (known today as katsina figures) and ceremonial dancers in decorative work also increased at this time. Those making such images usually tried to conventionalize their appearance to make them deliberately inaccurate, and thus less offensive to the natives themselves; however, these attempts still were subject to disapproval by natives and non-natives alike. During the 1950s, Navajo smiths introduced a generic silver kachina figure that became a popular form for mass production purposes, particularly after the introduction of spin casting around 1960. The leaf and foliate motifs found on silverwork made by the Navajo Platero family was also easily copied into centrifugal molds for manufacturing. A new wave of tour-

7.16. Cover of the July 1950 *Arizona Highways* issue with seminal information on Hopi overlay jewelry. Reprinted with permission from *Arizona Highways* magazine. *Courtesy of Robert Bauver.*

ism was set off by the Spring 1960 dedication and opening of the Navajo peoples' Monument Valley Tribal Park. Tourist work sought to capture the essence of the "Southwestern experience." As a result, new designs featuring petroglyphs and subjects from the regional landscape appeared. However, native artists had a way of making fun of dubious Indian kitsch; humor—and even irony—can be seen in some pieces from the 1950s and early 1960s (**7.17**, **7.18**). The opening of Disneyland in Anaheim, California, in 1955 would be followed in less than ten years by sly Zuni inlay renditions of Disney characters (**7.19**).

7.17. Navajo tourist buckle with Santa Fe Railroad motif, turquoise and coral stones, 1950s or 1960s. *Courtesy of Marianne and Bob Kapoun.*

7.18. Some playful Santo Domingo creations, ca. 1960s: a peace sign ring and unusual crushed stone buttons. *Courtesy of Marianne and Bob Kapoun.*

7.19. Three tourist era rings, 1950s–early 1960s; left to right: Apache *Gan* dancer, flowerpot, Mickey Mouse with turquoise necklace. *Courtesy of Marianne and Bob Kapoun.*

Jewelry-making in the 1950s reflected trends both old and new. Many traders and Indian arts experts actively endorsed "a freezing of older styles" to please collectors and dealers.[2] They urged renewed reliance on the heavy, simple designs of earlier decades. Jewelry made in the guilds also tended to be fairly conservative in look; such pieces were created to satisfy established tastes and guarantee steady sales. Certainly, the Indian-arts tourist industry depended on products with a known identity, yet novelty items could also be introduced to stimulate sales. In fact, at this same time, forces were in motion that fostered creativity. Turquoise and other favored materials (such as coral and shell) were more readily available in the 1950s, and their abundance triggered expanded variations in lapidary design. Satisfying substitutions also gained ground, as in the increased demand for coral-colored glass beads. Simply put, there was now more to work with—in terms of materials, techniques, styles, and even motifs—than ever before. The 1950s became, in effect, an "era of free experimentation."[3] With some Gallup traders and shops in regional cities taking orders for seasonably variable designs, there was a new impetus to create more and different types of jewelry and metalware. These efforts at variation were done to increase sales, since the local native economy did not reflect the same postwar boom experienced in other parts of the country—but the mood for experimentation, once achieved, was not lost. Native tastes for increased stonework were also being gratified. Native artisans across tribal lines attempted Zuni-style work with a variety of results. Smiths and lapidarists were creating items with a freshness and enthusiasm that became the first steps on the road to cross-tribal aesthetic exploration (later part of pan-Indianism) and artistic individualism.

Rumblings continued throughout the decade about the encroachment of fakes and manufactured Indian style jewelry on sales of the genuine product. An article on Hopi jewelry in a 1950 issue of *Arizona Highways* recommended that consumers obtain a list of reputable dealers from a local chamber of commerce (**7.16**). Cautionary articles appeared in such mainstream magazines as *Time* and *Travel* throughout 1954 warning visitors to the Southwest about bogus handicrafts, including imitation Indian jewelry. Tourist and consumer advice for those wanting to buy authentic handmade Indian jewelry appeared with greater frequency. Would-be purchasers were told to look for: silver items showing neat solder marks; lean, regular stamping and surface details; and signs of irregular color or streaks on the turquoise, indicating that the stones could have been boiled in paraffin or soaked in oil to enhance their look. An overall warning was that all pieces should be carefully finished. These cautions were necessary to warn consumers about knockoffs pouring out of factories, many of which were in Japan and Southeast Asia. The refitting of machinery from wartime mass production also added to the increase of assembly-line goods within the United States. "Liquid silver"— fine gauge silver tubular beads invented by the Rosetta family of Santo Domingo in the late 1950s— was rapidly copied into manufactured counterfeits.[4] The United Indian Traders Association began providing paper labels imprinted with the words "Indian Hand Made In _____ ", with the blank space for the location, to be filled in by the trader.

One of the most fundamentally important changes of the 1950s was the naming of individual native jewelers and their association with a given style or technique. Several significant developments illustrate this new emphasis. In 1952, the Los Angeles County Museum purchased silverwork made by the White Hogan silversmiths Kenneth Begay and Allen Kee. Unlike in the 1941 exhibition at the Museum of Modern Art in New York, in the 1958 "Southwest Indian Arts" exhibition at the California Palace of the Legion of Honor in San Francisco the works were identified by artist. The exhibition's catalogue states that selection was based on "artistic merit alone." Jewelry depicted includes a cast silver bracelet by Charles Loloma, a double-strand squash blossom necklace by Sadie Etsitty, and a turquoise and silver pin by Kemp Kushena. "Southwest Indian Arts II," held in 1965 at the California Palace, displayed works by Kenneth Begay and Myra Tucson. Mentions of individual jewelry-makers occur more frequently as the decade progressed. Navajo smith Mike Carroll came to work at the White Hogan during 1951-1952, after entries of his work gained notice at the Gallup Inter-tribal Ceremonial. Navajo smiths Luke Yazzie and Victor Begay received attention for their strong cluster work pieces. Zunis working with the cluster style included Donald Waseta, Simon Wallace, Warren Ondelacy, and Ondelacy's daughter Alice Quam. Two Pueblo smiths, Joe H. Quintana (Cochiti) and Julian Lovato (Santo Domingo), also garnered career boosts from non-native appreciation of their talent.

7.20. Two turquoise pins: on left, Zuni petitpoint floral shape; on right, Navajo cluster, 1920s or 1930s (with styles that were repeated throughout the 1950s and 1960s). *Courtesy of Lynn D. Trusdell, Crown & Eagle Antiques, Inc.*

7.21. Detail of Zuni petitpoint pin. *Courtesy of Lynn D. Trusdell, Crown & Eagle Antiques, Inc.*

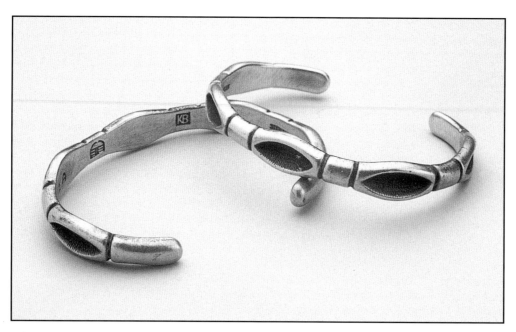

7.22. Bracelet guards, Kenneth Begay, Navajo, ca. 1940s. *Museum of Indian Arts and Culture/ Laboratory of Anthropology, Museum of New Mexico. Photography by Blair Clark.*

7.23. Set of tools once used by Sam Bahe, Navajo smith, active mid-twentieth century: small male and female die and punches, cold chisel, and mallet. *Courtesy of Micky and Dolly VanderWagen.*

Two men in particular mark the new shift in Southwestern Indian jewelry creation and its vision. Kenneth Begay (Navajo, 1913-1977) and Charles Loloma (Hopi, 1921-1991) stand as the most innovative and influential native jewelers of the twentieth century. This assessment is universally endorsed, not just because of the jewelry they made, but also in their roles as educators and role models. Begay had begun actively fabricating jewelry in the late 1930s, but a decade later, both he and Loloma had made creative contributions that were part of the changes that mark the 1950s and 1960s. Begay started as a blacksmith; he learned silversmithing from Fred Peshlakai, who possessed a direct link to the first generation of Navajo smiths. Begay's groundbreaking silver designs made while he worked at the White Hogan shop (first in Flagstaff, and then by 1950, in Scottsdale); these works are characterized by Begay's own hallmark of his initials, and a small stamp of a hogan (**7.22**). He taught many young jewelers—including his son Harvey (a future fine art jeweler)—through apprenticeships and demonstrations, and from 1968 to 1973 the elder Begay was a metalsmithing instructor at Navajo Community College in Many Farms, Arizona. Begay never stopped referring to older Navajo designs; in 1976 he was quoted as saying, "I keep looking at the old jewelry to get ideas about how things were put together."[5] Yet his works exude a modern, more strictly contemporary sense than most silverwork made at this time (**7.26**, **7.27**, **7.28**).

7.24. Large male and female dies, punches, and small blanks for naja and decorative appendages for a jewelry piece, mid-twentieth century. *Courtesy of Micky and Dolly VanderWagen.*

7.25. Tools of the trade: a white-gas blowtorch from ca. 1958, later replaced by butane and acetylene torches; a heating grate (mid-twentieth century), on which a jewelry piece was placed so that it could be heated over coals while a smith used a bellows. On the wood stump is an anvil made from a railroad iron rail. *Courtesy of Micky and Dolly VanderWagen.*

7.26. Two silver hammered and incised bracelets by Kenneth Begay from the 1950s. *Courtesy of Martha Hopkins Struever.*

7.27. Belt with seven silver conchas and rectangular buckle by Kenneth Begay, made late 1950s. *Courtesy of Martha Hopkins Struever.*

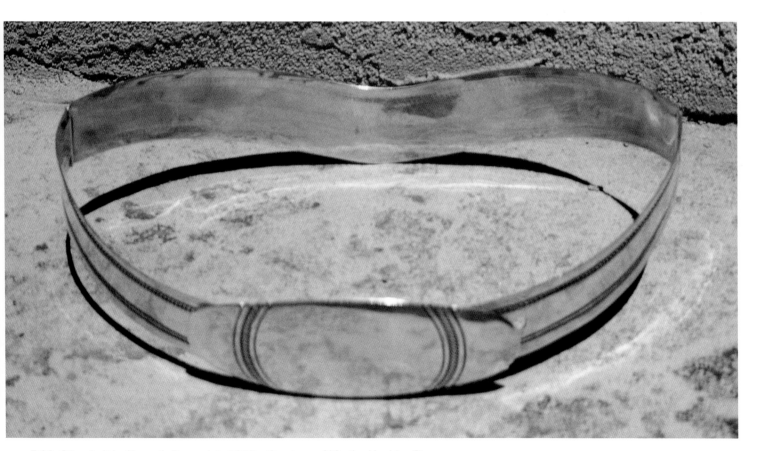

7.28. Silver belt by Kenneth Begay, late 1960s. *Courtesy of Martha Hopkins Struever.*

Loloma studied art at Alfred University in 1947, where he received formal studio training in design and color. In addition to his jewelry work, he was a successful painter and potter. His jewelry-making in the 1950s explored traditional tufa casting and the mainstream lost-wax casting process. Loloma's unique fabrications, including his "hidden designs" (additional designs on the inside of his bracelets, pendants, and other pieces, a technique he first conceived around 1962-1965), and unusual lapidary innovations, brought him remarkable public recognition (**7.29**, **7.30**). He experimented with gold as early as 1953, demonstrating its viability as a jewelry material in native creations. Loloma also personalized his design choices, as in his adoption of the badger paw motif from his own clan emblem (**7.31**). His jewelry was even privately exhibited overseas in Paris in 1963—the world capital of avant-garde design at that time, and a tribute to the direction his works were increasingly taking (**7.32**). Loloma taught at various venues during the late 1950s; his most influential position came from 1962 to 1965, as instructor in Plastic Arts and Marketing at the new Institute of American Indian Arts (IAIA) in Santa Fe. (Note the importance of marketing to the college's curriculum.) Yet Loloma, like Begay, also used older jewelry as a critical reference point.[6] Both Begay and Loloma represented a new identity for the individual Southwestern Indian jewelry-maker: master silversmith and lapidarist, design innovator, and true artist.

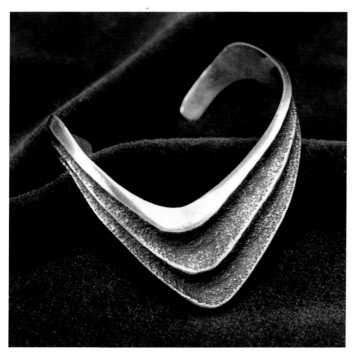

7.29 Sandcast V-shaped bracelet with textured surface by Charles Loloma, late 1960s. *Courtesy of Martha Hopkins Struever.*

7.30 Sandcast cuff bracelet by Charles Loloma, made around 1965–1970. *Courtesy of Martha Hopkins Struever.*

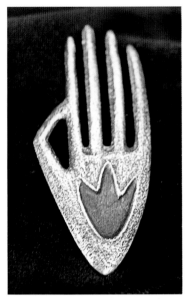

7.31. Badger paw ring of sandcast silver by Charles Loloma, late 1960s. *Courtesy of Martha Hopkins Struever.*

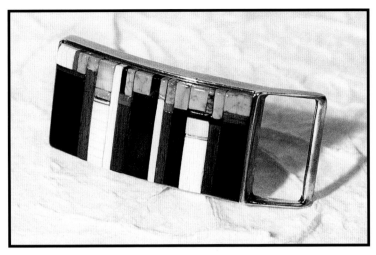

7.32. Rectangular buckle with inlaid stone rows, by Charles Loloma, Hopi, 1970s. *Courtesy of Carol and John Krena.*

7.33. Large Zuni inlay bolo depicting a Plains Indian riding a buffalo, with jet, shell, abalone and turquoise, late 1950s–early 1960s. *Courtesy of Lynn D. Trusdell, Crown & Eagle Antiques, Inc.*

These thoughtful, articulate artists produced works that were models for a new category of adornment within the Indian arts industry by the 1970s: fine art jewelry. These works, a fashionable commodity in keeping with more prosperous times, brought renewed consumer interest in collecting contemporary pieces. The 1960s were a period when Southwestern natives sought solidarity through such diverse activities as legal battles against states, powwows, and increased tribal intermarriage. There was dissatisfaction with conditions on the reservation, economic and bureaucratic shortcomings, and the plight of Indians living in urban areas; all these factors stirred social activism, including the new and controversial American Indian Movement (AIM). Families with a tradition of making arts continued as they had previously, but they also eagerly sought new educational opportunities. More natives now pursued art studies outside of the Indian schools. Nevertheless, a powerful development in the educational growth process was the establishment in 1962 of the IAIA, a two-year college. Young native students entering the college had a chance to follow a curriculum that instilled pride in indigenous cultures, and their course work was presided over by a distinguished faculty that included such challenging educators and artists as Lloyd Kiva New, Loloma, Allan Houser, and Jimmy Yazzie. The instructors encouraged the fledgling spirit of pan-Indianism through cross-cultural explorations as a means to achieve new artistic expression. Navajo and Pueblo jewelry creation would soon impact on the work of students from other cultural groups. By the mid-1960s, Southwestern Indian jewelry held a leadership position within the Indian arts industry, in terms of sales and public appeal.

7.34. Turquoise floral style earrings, 1950s or 1960s, probably Zuni. *Courtesy of Micky and Dolly VanderWagen.*

7.35. Inlay pin of a Hopi girl, Zuni or Hopi, 1950s–1960s. *Author's collection.*

7.36. Cluster work turquoise bracelet in a style popular at Zuni in the 1950s. *Author's collection.*

7.37. Tortoise shell bolo slide of Apache Mountain dancer (*Gan*); hallmark of maker Elliot Qualo, Zuni, 1960s. *Courtesy of Micky and Dolly VanderWagen.*

7.38. Tubular coral beads, drilled in Italy and imported, with old pump-drilled green ear-bobs attached; ear string added later, 1950s. *Courtesy of Robert Bauver.*

7.39. Inlay pin of two rearing horses, by Frank Vacit, Zuni, 1940s (formerly in the collection of C.G. Wallace). *Courtesy of Carol and John Krena.*

7.40. Isleta cross necklace of the late nineteenth century, with glass trade beads. *Courtesy of Carol and John Krena.*

7.41. A detail of Isleta cross, late nineteenth century. *Courtesy of Carol and John Krena.*

7.42. Necklace of coral glass beads with revival style dragonfly pendant by Mike Bird-Romero, San Juan, made ca. 1995. *Courtesy of the artist. Author's collection.*

Below:
7.43. Detail of dragonfly cross pendant on Bird-Romero's necklace. *Courtesy of the artist. Author's collection.*

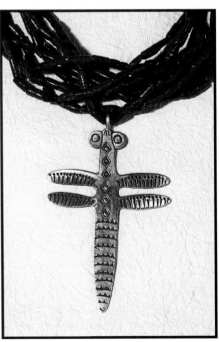

* * *

The mid-1960s serve as an appropriate historical dividing line between native-made jewelry of the past and that belonging to a new and exciting future. This transition can be confirmed in the shared perception of today's artists and consumers that this older jewelry has an enduring artistic legacy. Before the 1960s, Southwestern Indian jewelry was viewed as craft work because it seemed to possess the craft elements of traditional presentation, continuity in basic appearance, and anonymous creation. Ironically, these qualities were inherently false. Silver and turquoise native jewelry produced since the 1860s was far from traditional (in fact, it came from, and borrowed from, other cultures), was continuously changing, and was made by individuals who were anonymous only because it suited the non-native Indian arts industry to present them as such. The dark shadow cast by manufactured imitation Indian jewelry also reduced formal recognition of the genuine article's artistic nature. Additionally, native jewelry made between 1940 and 1970 has been historically undervalued by collectors because the status inherent in "antique" pieces has overshadowed the more "recent" pieces.

Aside from its "antique" appeal, the unique, cross-culturally derived adornment made by nineteenth-century smiths—laboring with rough tools and great ingenuity—became prized commodities precisely because these items possessed expressive artistic qualities. Even the tugs and pulls of the twentieth-century Indian jewelry industry could not restrain this artistic impulse. Over time, the continued use of innovation and fine design made jewelry from progressive decades desirable as well. Any doubters have only to look at the range of jewelry illustrated in chronological order throughout these chapters to see that these winning qualities—qualities that define an art form—were always in place. The ultimate tribute comes from native jewelers of the 1970s through 1990s who proudly refer back to older jewelry, and who may create revival styles in honor of this work. What makes the first one hundred years of Navajo and Pueblo jewelry creation so formative is this jewelry's power to affect current and future design, and that contemporary jewelers pay homage to the potent artistry of those who came before (**7.40-7.43**).

[1]Paula A. Baxter, "Navajo and Pueblo Jewelry," p. 39.
[2]David Neumann, "Modern Developments in Indian Jewelry," *El Palacio* 57 (June 1950): 175-176.
[3]Paula A. Baxter, "Navajo and Pueblo Jewelry," p. 38.
[4]Carl Rosnek and Joseph Stacey, *Skystone and Silver: The Collector's Book of Southwest Indian Jewelry* (Englewood Cliffs, NJ: Prentice-Hall, 1976), pp. 116-117.
[5]Ibid., p. 120.
[6]Ibid., pp. 107-109.

Chapter 8.
What Collectors Need to Know

Buying and collecting older Southwestern Indian jewelry can be exciting and satisfying. A remarkable number of beautiful works are on view in museums, at gallery exhibitions, and specialized antique Indian arts shows (**8.1**). Many items of a rare and historically significant nature remain in private collections. Collectors are drawn to a wide range of physical and aesthetic factors. Some people enjoy the luster and feel of coin or ingot silver. Others revel in the color and texture of turquoise, shell, and semiprecious stones that are found on some pieces. For many people, there is simple pride in owning adornment has been made by and worn by Native Americans from an earlier era. Some people buy items for personal wear (like the author), while others re

8.1. Rio Grande Pueblo necklace, length 12½ inches.
School of American Research, Catalog Number IAF. S20.

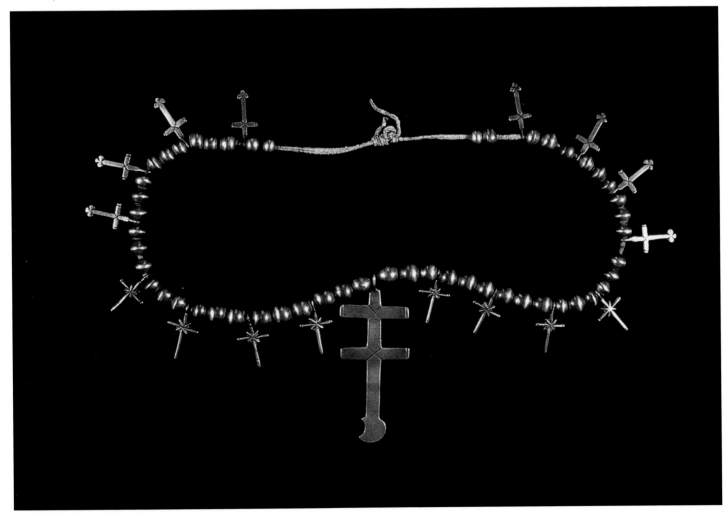

serve pieces for private display or for investment purposes. Yet at the heart of most collecting decisions is the question: "Is this object the real thing?" Consumers should take time to study this older jewelry and its physical properties, and to compare such work with items made at a later date. It is safe to say that most collectors have had at least one disappointing experience, particularly at the start of their collecting career (**8.2**). Some would-be collectors have been unnecessarily discouraged. Additionally, many experts in the antique Indian arts field admit that they themselves have been misled at one time or another.

8.2. A fake: the author bought this piece in the belief that it was a Navajo-made cross pendant from 1910; the sheet silver is from a much later date, and the signs of wear are unconvincing. *Author's collection.*

The collecting game becomes even more enjoyable when players gain self-confidence. The same rules apply for purchasing pre-1970 native jewelry as in other areas: buy what you like, and pay only what seems to be a fair market price. However, it is still primarily a seller's market with older Indian jewelry, due to the relative scarcity of good, authentic pieces. Bargains are few and far between. True "old pawn" is extremely hard to find, and pawn tickets on a piece might not be a sign of the item's real origins. The would-be collector should devise his or her own course of self-education. This chapter lays out the means for such personal study.

Determining Authenticity

Knowing the historical background of an art object adds to its value. However, many times the history of a specific piece is virtually impossible to determine. Such a history is known as the *provenance* of the piece: this may be best defined as the documentation of an object from its creation to the present, including information about the object's ownership. Most collectors prize acquisitions that have a documented history, and the existence of a provenance will increase the value of an item. Information about a work's provenance is also valuable for scholarly purposes. Unfortunately, the vast majority of older Indian jewelry on the market cannot be authenticated so easily.

Another term of significance applied to some older jewelry is *pawn* or *old pawn*. The term, however, is frequently misunderstood and therefore misused. Native Americans placed their jewelry in pawn, usually with a trader at a trading post; this transaction allowed the jewelry to be held as collateral for advanced loans, or in trade for other hard goods. The pawn system dates to the early years of Southwestern Indian jewelry creation, and is still in effect on the Navajo reservation and in towns on the reservation's borders. Jewelry could also be held in pawn for safekeeping until needed for special occasions. This is active pawn, and traders and shopkeepers know not to sell these items: their owners plan to reclaim their jewelry at a future time. Unredeemed pawn items can be sold after a fixed time, or when the trader knows that there is no ownership claim in effect; this becomes *dead pawn*, and such pieces can enter the marketplace legitimately. For a long time, older jewelry has been called *old pawn*: it can be defined as pieces which had originally been made for and worn by native owners. However, some dealers and traders in the antique Indian arts field have used the terms old pawn and dead pawn interchangeably, thereby muddying the original meanings. Over the years, sellers have exploited the native-made and used context of pawn to attract sales from tourists and collectors. There is also disagreement about the cut-off date for genuine old pawn: some experts argue for 1899, when commercial influence first started, as one end date; others offer either 1930 or 1940. In recent years, however, jewelry from the 1940s through 1960s has also been offered for sale at antique Indian arts shows. Many novice collectors and consumers have also been given the false impression that all old pawn is valuable or of good quality.

Reproductions of previously created art objects are a fact of life. In many cases, these copies are made for positive reasons, as learning experiences by practicing artists, or as tributes to the original object. Reproductions deliberately made to be passed off as originals are clearly *fakes* and *forgeries*. Sadly, the antique Indian arts market has its own share of this problem, one that haunts all the fine and decorative arts alike. Again, the real scarcity of authentic historical and artifactual items opens the door to unscrupulous forgers.

Opposite page:
8.3. An array of Navajo and Pueblo jewelry pieces with bird motifs: all silver, many with stamp work or turquoise settings, 1900s–1940s. *Courtesy of Lynn D. Trusdell, Crown & Eagle Antiques, Inc.*

8.4. Two birds: larger bird is coin silver with set stones, smaller piece shows traditional stamping decoration, mid-twentieth century. *Courtesy of Lynn D. Trusdell, Crown & Eagle Antiques, Inc.*

8.5. A ring popular with Zuni men in the 1930s and 1940s (note the deep green color that the untreated turquoise has turned), formerly from the collection of C.G. Wallace. *Author's collection.*

8.6. Two Zuni snake rings from green turquoise: large ring with ruby eyes was purchased in 1927; smaller ring made by Leekya Deyuse, 1930s or 1940s. *Courtesy of Robert Bauver.*

Allied to this issue is the concept of *misrepresentation*. If a dealer or seller knowingly attempts to offer a reproduction piece of jewelry as a genuine older object, and asks for a price in accordance with the worth of the original, then they are guilty of the twin sins of fraud and misrepresentation. It is also possible for someone unknowingly to misrepresent a reproduction as a legitimate old piece, based on a lack of knowledge of the object's origins and a misreading of its physical properties. The outcome is unfortunate for the buyer, nonetheless. Misrepresentation is also against the law as defined by the Indian Arts and Crafts Act of 1990 (Public Law 101-644), which covers all arts in both traditional and contemporary styles created after 1935. The enactment of this law indicates how serious and long-standing the problem of misrepresentation is in relation to modern native-made arts, including jewelry.

With this in mind, the thoughtful buyer or collector needs to be aware of the various types of commodities on offer in the marketplace. In addition to genuine handmade antique (defined here as pre-1940), older, and contemporary native-made jewelry, consumers should be aware of the following types of jewelry: replicas, composites, revival style, Indian style and Southwest style. Reproductions, sometimes called *replicas*, appear regularly; just as museum gift shops will feature reproductions (often mass manufactured) of notable original pieces from their collections, so certain kinds of Southwestern Indian jewelry have been copied. Older native-made jewelry on the market is also available in which parts of the piece have been repaired or replaced; such works may be referred to as *composite* pieces. Some contemporary native jewelers deliberately fabricate jewelry from a combination of old and new materials. As a practical solution, composites may be necessary; for example, when a fine quality older concha belt is intact, with the exception of one cracked concha plaque. The decision to restore or replace parts of an older piece of jewelry is often a good one. As long as a composite piece is not misrepresented as entirely original, such items are valid offerings.

Another category of note is *revival style* jewelry; these items are of recent creation and deliberately made in a form, style, or design of an earlier period. Many post-1970s fine art jewelers create such pieces in honor of works made by an older generation. Frequently, the materials used in a revival style piece betray its more recent origins. Revival style pieces are completely legitimate when they are portrayed and sold as

8.7. Twelve Navajo and Pueblo rings with turquoise settings, early twentieth century. *Courtesy of Lynn D. Trusdell, Crown & Eagle Antiques, Inc.*

8.8. Two *ketohs,* or bowguards, with silver cast cornstalk and steer head designs, Navajo, early twentieth century. *Courtesy of Lynn D. Trusdell, Crown & Eagle Antiques, Inc.*

8.9. A bar full of old Navajo and Pueblo bracelets, demonstrating the variety of styles used by native smiths in the early twentieth century. *Courtesy of Lynn D. Trusdell, Crown & Eagle Antiques, Inc.*

8.10. An early row bracelet made for the tourist trade, and now a popular collectible. As a result, buyers should watch out for recent reproductions and imitation pieces on the market that are based on Harvey House jewelry. *Author's collection.*

such. However, the line between a revival style work and a blatant forgery can be difficult; some of this depends on the viewer's expertise, and the quality of information relayed about the piece and its creation. Yet another pitfall lies in the existence of *Indian style* and *Southwest style* jewelry: consumers should know that these terms refer to jewelry that is not native-made. The proliferation of Southwest style jewelry in mail order catalogs and department stores' costume jewelry sections has created confusion for buyers in recent years. Many post-1970 native jewelers use a distinctive hallmark on their pieces to denote their work.

These various factors demonstrate how important it is to view and examine as much Southwestern Indian jewelry as possible. The most effective way to do this is to visit museums and gallery exhibitions that feature historical displays of jewelry, and attend specialized antique Indian arts auctions and sales. Would-be collectors should read as much literature as possible, and consult experts or more experienced collectors (who, alas, in many cases may also be competitors). It may be possible, as the result of networking, and through friendships formed during collector-oriented activities, that the novice collector might receive the opportunity to view a private collection or obtain a private tour of a museum's permanent collection holdings.

It is logical that some of the most important collections of Southwestern Indian jewelry reside in that region. In New Mexico, great collections can be seen at a number of institutions. In Albuquerque, there is the Maxwell Museum of Anthropology at the University of New Mexico. Santa Fe has the School of American Research, the Museum of Indian Arts and Culture, and the Wheelwright Museum; in that city there are also exhibitions at the museum of the Institute of American Indian Arts. The Millicent Rogers Museum in Taos has an outstanding permanent exhibition of older Navajo and Pueblo jewelry, based on the founder's own dedicated collecting.

Arizona's Museum of Northern Arizona (Flagstaff) and the Hopi Cultural Center (on Second Mesa) possess the country's finest holdings of older Hopi jewelry and examples of the Hopi overlay style. In Phoenix, the Heard Museum has remarkable permanent collection items on display and features important exhibitions. Jewelry also appears in exhibitions at the Arizona State Museum in Tucson and the Amerind Institute in Dragoon.

Significant holdings of Southwestern Indian jewelry are found in museums in other areas of the United States as well. Other major museums that have featured displays of older Southwestern jewelry include the following:

Denver Museum of Natural History, Denver, Colorado;

Southwest Museum, Los Angeles, California;

California Institute of Arts and Sciences, San Francisco, California;

Field Museum, Chicago, Illinois;

Eiteljorg Museum, Indianapolis, Indiana;

Museum of Archaeology and Anthropology, University of Pennsylvania, Philadelphia, Pennsylvania;

Montclair Art Museum, Montclair, New Jersey;

Thaw Collection, Fenimore House, New York Historical Society, Cooperstown, New York;

Brooklyn Museum, Brooklyn, New York;

the anthropology museums of Yale and Harvard Universities.

In addition, the combined collections of the Heye Foundation and the National Museum of the American Indian, with venues in New York and (by 2003) Washington, D.C., hold the promise of important exhibitions to come.

Finally, the role of experts in guiding collecting choices cannot be underestimated. Good quality older Southwestern Indian jewelry will not be inexpensive. Most collectors wish not only to buy well and wisely, but to pay appropriate prices for their acquisitions. Developing a relationship with one or more expert dealers aids the education process and provides the collector with a reliable source for purchases. Experts arrive at their knowledge through a variety of experiences; many often specialize in particular types of antique Indian goods, and they represent their skills accordingly. Authentication is a serious practice, especially for those individuals offering their services as appraisers. Indian traders are one category of experts; but the number of truly experienced individuals raised in the Indian arts business is rapidly decreasing. In many cases, the most reputable traders come from multi-generation trading families, with roots in a particular area of the Southwest. Good reputations are earned over time; reliable traders gather their own following of dedicated buyers and collectors. The same rule holds true for those traders who tour various regions of the United States, holding sales shows in hotels and community halls. There are two societies devoted to ethical selling practices and concern for consumer education. These groups contain members who run retail stores, galleries, or personal consulting services:

Antique Tribal Art Dealers Association (ATADA)
www.atada.org
Indian Arts and Crafts Association (IACA)
www.iaca.com

Both societies hold sales shows for wholesalers and individual customers at set times of the year; these venues are dependable sources for viewing goods and making purchases. Their websites offer the most up-to-date address, membership, and association staff information. Most serious collectors develop working relationships with reputable dealers over time. This practice aids buyers and collectors in their educational process and greatly reduces opportunities for disappointment.

8.11. Navajo early style square buckle, ca. 1900. *Courtesy of Cynthia and Robert Gallegos.*

8.12. This pre-1970 bracelet is set with turquoise from the King's Manassa mine in Nevada. *Author's collection.*

8.13. A tufa block with a cut-out design for sandcasting, early to mid-twentieth century. *Courtesy of Micky and Dolly VanderWagen.*

8.14. Four large cut and shaped stones of Morenci turquoise. *Courtesy of Micky and Dolly VanderWagen.*

Conservation and Care

Older Southwestern Native American jewelry will show signs of overt or subtle wear. These telltale marks are frequently used by experts to determine authenticity, and sometimes the age of the object as well (**8.11**). Other clues can be learned from the cuts of stones, types of mounts, chemicals used, and the choice of materials for fabrication (**8.12**). Certain types of markings can determine whether an object is made from a sandcast mold or is the product of mechanical spin casting (**8.13**). Many pieces made from silver, even those from the earliest decades of native silversmithing, can be remarkably sturdy. Works made predominantly of shell and stone, however, can be vulnerable to the forces of time: these pieces may pull loose from their inlay setting or easily become chipped. Turquoise has its own strengths and weaknesses, too: cracked edges, tiny fault lines, and insecure settings can cause structural damage to the stone.

Conservation and care of such materials depends on their owners' intentions. The repair and replacement of weak or missing parts can affect the object's original value. If the jewelry is meant for personal wear, some basic strengthening of the piece is a practical step, but objects that have a truly artifactual nature should not be altered; instead, items require proper storage, preferably in waterproof, airtight containers, and they should be carefully wrapped and not placed too close to other items.

The decision whether to store or display older jewelry is a personal one, based on a variety of individualistic factors. Such a decision can also be made by consulting an expert. The fineness of silver used in creating a piece will determine its tensile strength; some items, such as cuff bracelets, can crack or be malformed if handled roughly. Heavy wear can thin the silver on the shanks of rings and cause stress on solder lines or metal fastenings. Decorations incised or embossed on a silver piece can also be worn down by years of wear. Jewelry exposed to liquids, pollutants, or other agents will suffer similar deterioration. It is important to remember that many native peoples wore their jewelry actively, and not just for special events. So for many collectors, signs of wear are a badge of honor. The most common signs of wear on older jewelry are rough edges, thin patches on silver, chipped shell and stone beads, and inlay or carved stones with cracks or nicks.

Cleaning such materials calls for care. Shell and stone do not react well to soap and water; washing with such liquids can also loosen the epoxy backing from stone settings. Most dealers and traders do not recommend using liquid polishes. A jeweler's rouge cloth is the best tool for cleaning and polishing silver. Oxidation that has been worn away can be restored by a liver of sulphur compound; this is best done by jewelers familiar with Indian jewelry. Most mainstream jewelry repair stores do not have staff who understand the materials used in native-made jewelry, especially on older pieces: they can do permanent damage to such objects. ATADA and IACA dealers know reliable sources for such repair or restoration work. Many of these dealers work with silversmiths or jewelers who specialize in this type of repair. There are also individuals who advertise in trade publications related to the Indian arts business, such as the *Indian Trader*, who may be consulted for expert repairs. It may not always be necessary to send jewelry to the Southwest for repair, but this course is preferable to choosing a local shop that might damage the piece.

8.15. Box of small cut stones from #8 Spiderweb turquoise. *Courtesy of Micky and Dolly VanderWagen.*

Simply knowing the components of a piece of jewelry can help the owner take care of it. Collectors should attempt to learn the differences between treated, or chemically enhanced, turquoise and natural turquoise. Old cuts of turquoise that have not been treated will fade over time, usually into a deep green color. Imitation turquoise, in forms from paste to plastic block or cake, appeared in the later 1930s to the present (**8.16**). Most modern turquoise that has been treated is known as *stabilized:* chemical binders are added to provide a desired color, texture, or firmness. Many of the materials used for modern native jewelry-making have been stabilized, including coral; this treatment does make the piece more durable (**8.17**). But jewelry made before these techniques is more delicate; rough handling is more likely to cause significant damage to stonework.

One word on a topic related to care—security. Collectors who amass valuable pieces should check with their insurance carriers to see about the need for appraisal and additional coverage. Insurance agents and other professionals can advise individuals about secure storage as well. There are thieves around with a good working knowledge of the value of antique Indian arts, including jewelry. Those living in regions outside the Southwest should not be lulled into thinking that burglars will consider these pieces to be costume jewelry. After all, everyone has access to eBay and the *Antiques Road Show!*

8.16. Blue turquoise and lapis plastic block used to make imitation stones for modern jewelry. *Courtesy of Steven and Mary Delzio.*

8.17. Pieces of plastic block or "cake" available on the market today. Block can be used as a substitute for genuine turquoise, malachite, sugilite, coral, and lapis; it is also an important element in modern repair of older lapidary work. *Courtesy of Micky and Dolly VanderWagen.*

8.18. Small plastic "turquoise" stones for jewelry setting: a post-1940s development in active use today. *Courtesy of Micky and Dolly VanderWagen.*

Opposite page:
8.19. Turquoise can be extremely difficult to photograph accurately: this necklace of the 1940s, with leaves of Cripple Creek turquoise carved by Zuni master Leekya Deyuse, possesses an unique green tint that cannot be reproduced despite many attempts. *Private collection.*

8.20. Tumbled nuggets of Fox turquoise, probably mined in the 1970s. *Courtesy of Robert Bauver.*

Literature on Older Southwestern Indian Jewelry and Its Influence on Collectors and the Market

Books and other publications are important tools for learning about older jewelry. Non-native writers predominate this literature, thereby reflecting their own interests and expectations. Ethnographers working in the American Southwest usually gave more emphasis to pottery and weaving, with jewelry-making firmly relegated to an arts and crafts category (**8.21**). Archaeological excavations that yielded jewelry proved useful to native jewelry-makers, when illustrations of ancient works were included (**8.22**). By the 1950s, a body of writing emerged that focused largely on tourist and collector concerns. Thanks to studies by Washington Matthews, John Adair, and Arthur Woodward, much is known about the early years of Navajo and Pueblo silversmithing. However, more recent literature has concentrated on the work of fine art and contemporary jewelers.

8.21. "Drilling Turquoises," from James Stevenson's *Illustrated* Catalogue *of the Collections obtained from Zuni and Walpi...* 1885. *Author's collection.*

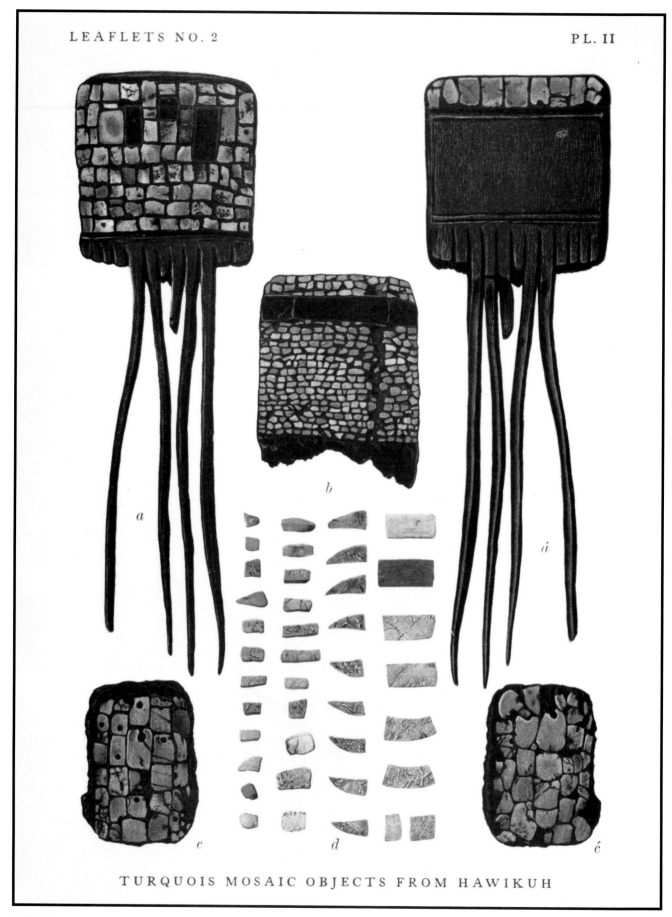

8.22. "Turquois Mosaic Objects from Hawikuh," from F.W. Hodge's
Turquois Works of Hawikuh. 1921. *Author's collection.*

8.23. Postcard for tourists, early to mid-twentieth century, showing native jewelry-making and wearing. *Courtesy of Robert Bauver.*

H-2451   NAVAHO INDIAN SILVERSMITH, N. M.   Copr. Fred Harvey.

A variety of magazine articles, reports, and some key books helped to shape collector interests, and are influential even today. In addition to the regional magazines, *Arizona Highways* and *New Mexico Magazine,* are museum and academic anthropological journals such as *El Palacio, Plateau,* and *The Kiva* (see **Bibliography**). Articles on jewelry have appeared in *American Indian Arts Magazine* since its start in 1975. Adair's classic study, *The Navajo and Pueblo Silversmiths,* was published initially in 1944 and has gone through a number of reprintings. This work was amplified by a book that appeared in 1973 by a librarian, Margery Bedinger, *Indian Silver; Navajo and Pueblo Jewelers.* The 1970s became a "boom" decade that triggered even more intense collector interest, and brought more publications. Trader C.G. Wallace placed part of his renowned collection up for sale in 1975; the sales catalog from Sotheby Parke Bernet, for the most part, is a good source for information and images on early jewelry designers and their work. Perhaps the most popular treatment of collector interests arrived in 1976: Carl Rosnek and Joseph Stacey's *Skystone and Silver: The Collector's Book of Southwest Indian Jewelry*; this work's real strength is in its interviews with important artists, dealers, and museum professionals who evaluate the Indian jewelry industry of the 1970s. Another important source of documentation comes in the form of three highly informative museum exhibition and permanent holdings catalogs that describe the collections of Fred Harvey (1981), Virginia Doneghy (1982), and Charles de Young and Ruth Elkus (1984) (see **Bibliography**).

However, two books in a series (even though they are widely separated in time) have had a powerful impact on those who collect older native-made jewelry. Dr. H.P. Mera's *Indian Silverwork of the Southwest, vol. 1* (1960), took a firm stand that pre-1930 silver made without elaborate stone settings was of higher quality than later pieces and styles. His book was followed by *Indian Silverwork of the Southwest, vol. 2* (1976) by Dale Stuart King; the author, slightly more liberal in his judgments, extended Mera's viewpoint to include jewelry made in the 1940s, 1950s, and 1960s. King's greatest concern was with the effects of the boom for turquoise and silver jewelry taking place in the mid-1970s. The value judgments made by Mera and King deeply affected the demand for certain types of older pieces. At the same time, the lack of attention paid to the good qualities and innovations of post-1940 jewelry meant that its collecting potential was bypassed.

Happily, the decades since the 1970s have brought new insights. Native American arts are now considered a robust aspect of material culture. Contemporary collectors and consumers better understand how Indian jewelry can be split into various kinds of commodities: as artifacts, costume jewelry, or even fine art. This enlarged perspective has challenged entrenched attitudes and has led to greater appreciation of current native jewelry-making. Certain styles launched after 1940 are the source for vigorous contemporary expressions (**8.24**, **8.25**). More recently, too, collectors can acquire a number of attractive picture books and price guides, the types of publications essential to consumer education. Thoughtfully published histories on Southwestern Indian jewelry, such as Allison Bird's *Heart of the Dragonfly*, have sparked collector interest in certain kinds of older jewelry. As more studies on the subject appear, this growing investigative literature will only aid the learning process.

8.24. These bangles from the early 1990s have their design roots in the Hopi overlay style of the 1940s. *Author's collection.*

8.25. Silver mask bracelet with a variety of raised inlaid stones and wood by Charles Loloma, made around 1980. *Courtesy of Martha Hopkins Struever.*

The Importance of Older Designs and Styles to Contemporary Native Jewelry

Southwestern Indian jewelry-making today is clearly a vital, living art. This can be seen at the displays and booths of the annual Indian arts shows, such as the Gallup Ceremonial and the Santa Fe Indian Market. Also visible is the active growth and change of jewelry forms, designs, and styles. Just as native peoples have had to adjust and adapt to modern society and its demands—a process known as acculturation—so do their decorative arts reflect these developments. In fact, throughout the one hundred years of jewelry creation surveyed in this book, the effects of acculturation and artistic accommodation are responsible for the aesthetically interesting variations that can be seen in the illustrations.

It is a natural temptation in our Western-oriented world to attach art historical labels to native-made art, but ultimately such actions are a disservice. Eventually the time will come for Native American historians themselves to evaluate the cumulative impact of Indian jewelry production. Until then, we should look again at this concept of the "living arts" and understand how acculturation has enriched jewelry design. For native peoples, their older arts are a prized artistic legacy, subject to respectful revivals or reinterpretations. This healthy interest in older jewelry forms and designs has been acknowledged by notable jewelers ranging from Kenneth Begay and Charles Loloma to today's young artists. The fine art jewelers of the 1970s and 1980s were quick to honor their predecessors, even as they devised innovative departures from such older work.

8.26. Two sets of earrings: on left, hoops with squash beads, pre-1900; on right, squash beads derived from earlier style, and used for sale to tourists, 1940s, on card from a trading post. *Courtesy of Lynn D. Trusdell, Crown & Eagle Antiques, Inc.*

The contemporary artist's study of older jewelry has been a valuable one. In turn, the appreciation of pre-1970 Indian jewelry by collectors and consumers often leads to a new regard for contemporary work. Many consumers therefore enjoy purchasing both types of adornment. Many collectors who actively wear their jewelry on a regular basis (such as the author), buy well-made contemporary pieces that have references to, or echoes of, older designs and styles, done as an affectionate tribute to the work of those who came before. Those individuals just beginning to buy or collect would also do well to consider the acquisition of pieces made in the 1950s and 1960s. In addition to being attractive, with interesting designs, more and more of this jewelry is showing up at antique Indian arts shows and sales. Because a greater volume of jewelry was made in the 1950s and 1960s, more pieces are available, often at more reasonable prices.

Appreciating the Product and Its Market

Think of older Southwestern Indian jewelry as a pyramid: at the top perch the earliest genuine items, which are now scarce, then the pyramid broadens out with each successive decade. Pre-1900 pieces command a strong price because of their scarcity, and the competition to own these works is intense. Jewelry from the early to mid-1900s is more plentiful, and these numbers swell even more after 1945. Collectors have an interesting range of commodities to choose from: original early work; tourist jewelry; or later handcrafted pieces displaying distinctive techniques and styles.

As the collector's eye and mind develops over time, that individual will develop a keen sense of what he or she likes. Buying decisions are based on highly personal factors, such as aesthetic judgment and taste. Therefore, this process is not a wholly rational one. Collectors can and do make mistakes, and preferences change over time or move in different directions. One approach for would-be collectors or consumers calls for evaluating potential acquisitions according to four key considerations: (1) materials; (2) quality of construction or craftmanship; (3) style or design; and (4) unique personal appeal.

8.27. "Navaho Youth" from Karl Moon, "Indian Studies—Grand Canyon, Arizona (1904–1910?)." *Photography Collection, Miriam and Ira D. Wallach Division of Art, Prints and Photographs. The New York Public Library. Astor, Lenox and Tilden Foundations.*

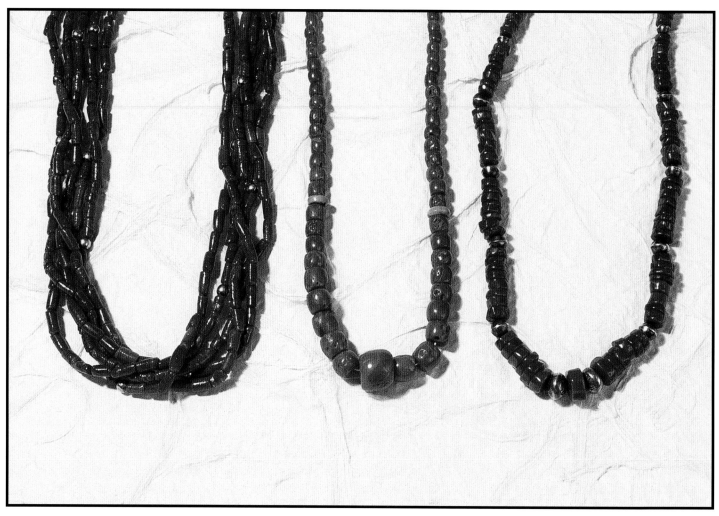

8.28. A variety of pre-1970 coral and imitation coral. From left to right: coral-colored glass trade beads; stabilized coral; oxblood coral beads with resin finish. *Author's collection.*

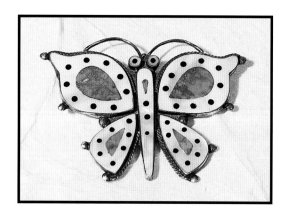

8.29. A Zuni inlay butterfly by Lambert Homer Jr. *Courtesy of Carol and John Krena.*

On the first two considerations: few collectors willingly purchase poorly-made pieces with inferior materials. Quality and good craftmanship are major factors; for example, if a piece lacking in these qualities is fragile or deteriorating, is the collector willing to plan and pay for the necessary restoration work? If such a piece fills a gap in a collection, possesses artifactual significance, or has a strong unique appeal, a collector might then overrule the first two considerations just listed. Concerning the third consideration: many people choose to collect specific jewelry styles or designs. This preference drives many collecting decisions, and people may acquire items according to favored lapidary styles (such as needlepoint or mosaic inlay) or certain designs such as animals or kachina figures (**8.29**). Often, the fourth consideration—unique personal appeal—is the strongest factor in collecting choices. This may include buying a piece because of its known provenance, known artist, or tribal affiliation. Some collectors may be drawn to acquiring specific jewelry forms, such as Navajo bracelets, Pueblo cross necklaces, or multi-part earrings (**8.30**).

Because collecting is a highly personal activity, individuals may find that their interests do not always remain consistent. The cornerstone to good collecting, as in other areas, is developing a working relationship with one or more reputable dealers. This principle extends also to venues for purchasing: the best place to do this is at established an-

8.30. Group of eight older-style Navajo bracelets with a variety of settings, 1900 to 1920. *Courtesy of Jay Evetts.*

tique Indian arts shows that attract quality dealers. A relationship between a collector and dealer or trader may bring beneficial side results; for example, it may be possible to trade in early purchases or "buying mistakes" as partial payment of a new acquisition, or in exchange for credit on a future purchase. Items bought in the first years of collecting, and now unwanted, may be useful to a dealer who will be able to sell them. The collector gains by divesting such pieces, and may possibly be able to build credit toward a more ambitious purchase. The overall experience gained by selecting, buying, and even reevaluating, objects for a collection allows the consumer a chance to grow and refine his or her taste.

Learning to be a good collector is a continually shifting and fascinating process. A practical wariness is essential. Bargains are exciting possibilities when they appear, but are fairly infrequent. Usually a canny dealer has already been there and left with the goods. The exciting new world of eBay and other on-line auction services is just the newest of many interesting ways to examine and possibly obtain older Indian jewelry. However, no one should pay a collector's price for a piece of costume jewelry (or worse). Taking the time to exercise good judgment in what you buy, and whom you obtain it from, will net you the best results of all. So with all this advice in mind—don't worry, buy what you like, and be happy!

8.31. A set of five Santo Domingo earrings in a variety of mid-twentieth-century styles. *Courtesy of Marianne and Bob Kapoun.*

8.32. Five rings displaying a variety of styles, from tourist designs to pieces that accentuate the abstract design power of silver and turquoise, early twentieth century. *Courtesy of Lynn D. Trusdell, Crown & Eagle Antiques, Inc.*

8.33. Group of bracelets and rings with snake motif, mostly Navajo with one piece signed "Wolfrobe" (probably Wolf Robe Hunt, Hopi), all 1900s to 1930s. *Courtesy of Lynn D. Trusdell, Crown & Eagle Antiques, Inc.*

Postscript

Like many people, I never intended to become a collector—it just happened. The passionate, giddy excitement of looking and buying has become so much more to me than just a hobby. I've discovered just how much being a collector can take over one's life: how it has affected my leisure time, vacations, and disposable income! Best of all, it has brought me into contact with a whole network of individuals involved in the field of Indian arts. I've made many wonderful acquaintances and some great friends.

Mostly, however, I think of those who came before. Nearly sixty years ago, Navajo and Pueblo men went to war on behalf of their country—a country which had not always treated them with fairness or given them the economic opportunities granted to so many others. Successive generations also heeded the call in later conflicts—Korea, Vietnam, and the Persian Gulf. There are times when I wear jewelry made by these men and their families that I feel a reflected sense of their creators' bravery and generosity. I am proud that these are the objects that I've chosen to gather, and to write about. It is very important that we honor our veterans, of all cultures. August 14 is Navajo Code Talkers Day.

P.A.B.

Appendix A
Jewelers Active before 1970 and Considered Important to the Antique Indian Arts Market

For a more extensive listing of artists, see *The Encyclopedia of Native American Jewelry* (see **Bibliography**) under Artist Name Index and separate entries by tribe or cultural group. This concise list of names was selected because of the frequency of their appearance as important figures in museum exhibitions and in sales advertisements, and because they currently command significant sales demand and prices in the marketplace.

Hopi
Willie Coin
Victor Coochwytewa
Bernard Dawahoya
Duwakuku
Bert Frederick
Fred Kabotie
Pierce Kewanwytewa
Charles Loloma
Lewis Lomay
Preston Monongye
Roscoe Narvasi
Earl Numkina
Allen Pooyama
Bert Puhuyestiwa
Morris Robinson
Harry Sakyesva
Lawrence Saufkie
Paul Saufkie
Emory Sekaquaptewa
Wayne Sekaquaptewa
Washington Talayumptewa
Tawanimptewa
Homer Vance

Navajo
Atsidi Chon
Kenneth Begay
Charlie Bitsui
Mose Blackgoat
Tom Burnsides
Mark Chee
Mike Carroll
Billie Goodluck
Hosteen Goodluck
Charlie Houck
John Hoxie
Wilfred Jones
Allen Kee
Fred Peshlakai
Frank Pinto
Ambrose Roanhorse
John Six
Roger Skeet
Slender Maker of Silver
Raymond Watson
Austin Wilson
Lee and Mary Yazzie
Chester Yellowhair

Rio Grande Pueblos
Diego Abeita
Vidal Aragon
Domingo Atencio
Ralph Atencio
Jose Jaramillo
Julian Lovato
Joe H. Quintana
Candido Romero
Ray and Mary Rosetta
Alfonso Roybal (Awa Tsireh)
Francisco Teyano

Zuni
Della Casa Appa
Juan Dedios
Leekya Deyuse
Disha
Virgil Dishta
Lambert Homer
Horace Iule
Mary Kallistewa
Kemp Kushena
John Gordon Leak
Leo Poblano
Alice Quam
Warren Quandelacy
Dan Simplicio
David Tsikewa
Myra Tucson
Ted Weahkee
Tom Weahkee
Zuni Dick
Bruce Zunie

Appendix B
Values Reference Guide

The market for older Southwestern Indian jewelry is subject to constant change. Prices will vary for a number of reasons, including geographic location and auction sales publicity. Certain types of jewelry, such as bola ties and concha belts, may sell better in the Southwest than in other regions. Some kinds of jewelry may also become more popular than others; these trends are not always easy to discern, but are usually reflected in the types of sales made at antique Indian arts shows or special auction sales.

True antique pieces, as well as unique pieces, will almost always command high prices. Collectors should expect to pay more for jewelry by notable older artists (see **Appendix A**), and for pieces that have a documented provenance. This guide lists the average prices for specific types of jewelry and their general time period. An average low price is given, followed by an average high price; these prices are meant to indicate the general low and high ranges, with the firm caveat that such prices can fluctuate over time, as with all goods subject to marketplace demand:

	Avg. low	Avg. high
Bola ties		
Navajo or Pueblo, pre-1970	$100	$700
Bracelets		
Hopi overlay, pre-1960	$250	$1,700
Navajo, silver or silver and stone, pre-1940	$350	$2,500
Navajo, silver and stone, 1940–1970	$175	$1,500
Pueblo, pre-1970	$250	$2,500
Concha belts		
Navajo or Pueblo, pre-1940	$750	$12,000
Navajo or Pueblo, 1940–1970	$600	$3,500
Dress ornaments; Navajo or Pueblo, pre-1970	$150	$500
Earrings		
Navajo or Pueblo, pre-1940	$250	$1,700
Navajo or Pueblo, 1940–1970	$100	$400

Necklaces

Navajo squash blossom, pre-1940	$1,400	$11,000
Navajo or Pueblo squash blossom, 1940–1970	$700	$1,500
Pueblo cross or cross pendant, pre-1940	$950	$4,500
Pueblo heishi (1 to 4 strands), pre-1940	$250	$1,700

Pins

Navajo or Pueblo, silver and stone, pre-1940	$250	$1,100
Navajo or Pueblo, silver and stone, 1940–1970	$95	$350
Zuni, inlay pin pendants under 3 in., pre-1940	$95	$550
Zuni, inlay pin pendants under 3 in., 1940–1970	$75	$350
Zuni, inlay pin pendants over 3 in., pre-1940	$325	$3,500
Zuni, inlay pin pendants over 3 in., 1940–1970	$250	$850

Rings

Navajo or Pueblo, pre-1940	$125	$500
Navajo or Pueblo, 1940–1970	$95	$350

Tourist era commercial jewelry, 1900–1970

	$75	$350

Auctions

The following sales auction prices have been included to give some idea of what kinds of older jewelry have been sold in recent years:

Named Artist

Leekya Deyuse, double-strand fetish necklace, 27 in. long. $3,025 (Allard Auctions, Santa Fe, NM, Aug. 15–16, 1999)

Leekya Deyuse, bear fetish necklace, 29 in. long. $5,500 (R.G. Munn, Albuquerque, NM, Feb. 5-7, 1999)

Charles Loloma, silver band bracelet with mosaic inlay, 25/8 in. wide. $11,500 (Sotheby's New York, Dec. 2, 1998)

Other

Navajo bracelet with two stamped carinated bands, five rectangular bezels of green turquoise, possibly ca. 1910–1915. $1,610 (Butterfield's, San Francisco, CA, June 21, 1999)

Navajo turquoise and shell necklace with two jaclas, 19¾ in. long. $600 (Christie's East, New York, Dec. 1, 1999)

Pueblo coral necklace, 15¼ in. long. $950 (Christie's East, New York, Dec. 1, 1999)

Navajo silver and hide belt, 43 in. long. $10,062 (Sotheby's New York, Dec. 4, 1997)

Bibliography

General History

Bailey, Garrick, and Roberta Glenn Bailey. *A History of the Navajos: The Reservation Years*. Santa Fe: School of American Research, 1986.

Bailey, Lynn Robison. *Bosque Redondo: The Navajo Internment at Fort Sumner, New Mexico, 1863-1868*. Tucson: Westernlore Press, 1998.

Dale, E.E. *The Indians of the Southwest: A Century of Development under the United States*. Norman: University of Oklahoma Press, 1949.

Dilworth, Leah. *Imagining the Primitive: Representations of Native Americans in the Southwest*. Washington, D.C.: Smithsonian Institution Press, 1996.

Dockstader, Frederick J. *Indian Arts of the Americas*. New York: Museum of the American Indian, Heye Foundation, 1973.

The Fabrics of Culture: The Anthropology of Clothing and Adornment. New York: Mouton, 1979.

Hewett, Edgar L. *Ancient Life in the American Southwest*. Indianapolis: Bobbs-Merrill, 1930.

Howard, Kathleen, and Diana Pardue. *Inventing the Southwest: The Fred Harvey Company and Native American Art*. Flagstaff: Heard Museum; Northland Publishing, 1996.

Huckel, John F. *First Families of the Southwest*. Kansas City, MO: Fred Harvey Company, 1916.

Kluckhohn, Clyde. *Navaho Material Culture*. Cambridge, MA: Belknap Press of Harvard University Press, 1971.

Krech, Shepard III, and Barbara A. Hall, eds. *Collecting Native America: 1870-1960*. Washington, D.C.: Smithsonian Institution Press, 1999.

Link, Martin A., ed. *Navajo: A Century of Progress, 1868-1968*. Window Rock, AZ: published by the Navajo Tribe, 1968.

Lummis, Charles F. *Mesa, Cañon, and Pueblo*. New York; London: Century, 1925.

McNitt, Frank. *The Indian Traders*. Norman: University of Oklahoma Press, 1962.

Paterek, Josephine. *Encyclopedia of American Indian Costume*. Denver: ABC-Clio, 1994.

Rockwell, David. *Giving Voice to Bear: North American Indian Rituals, Myths, and Images of the Bear*. Niwot, CO: Roberts Rinehart, 1991.

Sando, Joe S. *Pueblo Nations: Eight Centuries of Pueblo Indian History*. Santa Fe: Clear Light, 1992.

Schrader, Robert F. *The Indian Arts and Crafts Board: An Aspect of New Deal Policy*. Albuquerque: University of New Mexico Press, 1983.

Sturtevant, William C., gen. ed. *Handbook of North American Indians*. Washington, D.C.: Smithsonian Institution Press, 1978-1985. See esp. vols. 9 and 10, *Southwest*, both edited by Alfonzo Ortiz.

Trimble, Stephen. *The People: Indians of the American Southwest*. Santa Fe: School of American Research, 1993.

Underhill, Ruth M. *Life in the Pueblos*. Santa Fe: Ancient City Press, 1991.

Weigle, Marta, and Barbara A. Babcock, eds. *The Great Southwest of the Fred Harvey Company and the Santa Fe Railroad*. Phoenix: The Heard Museum, 1996.

Guides for Collectors

Bahti, Mark. *Collecting Southwestern Native American Jewelry*. New York: David McKay, 1980.

Bahti, Tom. *An Introduction to Southwestern Indian Arts and Crafts*. Las Vegas: KC Publications, 1973.

Baxter, Paula, with Allison Bird-Romero. *The Encyclopedia of Native American Jewelry*. Phoenix: Oryx Press, 2000.

Frank, Larry, with Millard Holbrook II. *Indian Silver Jewelry of the Southwest 1868-1930*. West Chester, PA: Schiffer Publishing, 1990.

Indian Arts and Crafts Association and Council for Indigenous Arts and Culture. *Collecting Authentic Indian Arts and Crafts: Traditional Work of the Southwest*. Summertown, TN: Book Publishing Company, 1999.

King, Dale Stuart. *Indian Silverwork of the Southwest*. Vol. 2. Tucson: Dale Stuart King, 1976.

Lund, Marsha. *Indian Jewelry: Fact and Fantasy*. Boulder: Paladin Press, 1976.

Mera, H.P. *Indian Silverwork of the Southwest*. Vol. 1. Tucson: Dale Stuart King, 1960.

Rosnek, Carl, and Joseph Stacey. *Skystone and Silver: The Collector's Book of Southwest Indian Jewelry*. Englewood Cliffs, NJ: Prentice-Hall, 1976.

Stacey, Joseph, ed. *Turquoise Blue Book and Indian Jewelry Digest*. Phoenix: Arizona Highways, 1975.

Turnbaugh, William A., and Sarah Turnbaugh. *Indian Jewelry of the American Southwest*. West Chester, PA: Schiffer Publishing, 1988.

Wright, Barton. *Hallmarks of the Southwest*. West Chester, PA: Schiffer Publishing, 1989.

Works on or Related to Jewelry

Adair, John. *The Navajo and Pueblo Silversmiths*. Norman: University of Oklahoma Press, 1944.

Anderson, Duane, ed. *The Legacy: Southwest Indian Art at the School of American Research*. Santa Fe: School of American Research, 1999.

Baxter, Paula A. "Native North American Art: Tourist Art." In *The Dictionary of Art*, edited by Jane Turner. London: Grove, 1996, vol. 22, pp. 667-670.

—————. "Navajo and Pueblo Jewelry, 1940-1970: Three Decades of Innovative Design Revisited." *American Indian Art Magazine* 21 (autumn 1996): 34-43.

—————. "Nineteenth-century Navajo and Pueblo Silver Jewelry." *The Magazine Antiques* 153, 1 (January 1998): 206-215.

Baxter, Sylvester. "An Aboriginal Pilgrimage." *Century Monthly Illustrated Magazine* 24 (August 1882): 526-536.

Bedinger, Margery. *Indian Silver: Navajo and Pueblo Jewelers*. Albuquerque: University of New Mexico Press, 1973.

Belknap, William. *Fred Kabotie, Hopi Indian Artist*. Flagstaff: Northland Press, 1977.

Bell, Barbara, and Ed Bell. *Zuni: The Art and the People*. 3 vols. Grants, NM: Squaw Bell Traders, 1975-1977.

Bennett, Edna Mae, and John Bennett. *Turquoise Jewelry of the Indians of the Southwest*. Colorado Springs, CO: Turquoise Books, 1973.

Bird, Allison. *Heart of the Dragonfly: The Historical Development of the Cross Necklaces of the Pueblo and Navajo Peoples*. Albuquerque: Avanyu Publishing, 1992.

Branson, Oscar T. *Fetishes and Carvings of the Southwest*. Tucson: Treasure Chest, 1976.

—————. *Indian Jewelry Making*. 2 vols. Tucson: Treasure Chest, 1977.

—————. *Turquoise: The Gem of the Centuries*. Tucson: Treasure Chest, 1975.

The C.G. Wallace Collection of American Indian Art, November 14, 15, and 16, 1975. Auction sales catalog. New York: Sotheby Parke-Bernet, 1975.

Cain, H. Thomas. *American Indian Jewelry*. Exhibition catalog. Phoenix: Heard Museum, 1966.

California Palace of the Legion of Honor. *Southwest Indian Arts*. Exhibition catalog. San Francisco: California Palace, 1958.

—————. *Southwest Indian Arts II*. Exhibition catalog. San Francisco: California Palace, 1965.

Chambliss, Catherine. "Metal of the Moon." *Arizona Highways* 17 (December 1941): 26-37.

Cirillo, Dexter. "Back to the Past: Tradition and Change in Contemporary Pueblo jewelry." *American Indian Art Magazine* 13 (spring 1988): 46-55+.

—————. *Southwestern Indian Jewelry*. New York: Abbeville Press, 1992.

Coe, Ralph T. *Lost and Found Traditions: Native American Art, 1965-1985*. Seattle: University of Washington Press, in assoc. with American Federation of Arts, 1986.

Colton, Mary-Russell F. "Hopi Silversmithing—Its Background and Future." *Plateau* 12 (July 1939): 1-7.

Conn, Richard. *A Persistent Vision: Art of the Reservation Days.* Exhibition catalog. Denver: Denver Art Museum, 1986.

————. *Robes of White Shell and Sunrise: Personal Decorative Arts of the Native American.* Exhibition catalog. Denver: Denver Art Museum, 1974.

Cowan, J.L. "Pueblo of Zuni." *Overland Monthly* 53 (April 1909): 280-285.

Dear, D.E. "On Jewelry Made in the Contemporary (U.S.A.) Style." *Leonardo* 12 (autumn 1979): 301-303.

Dimock, A.W. "Among the Navaho." *Outlook* 76 (February 6, 1904): 248-259.

Douglas, Frederic, and Rene D'Harnoncourt. *Indian Art of the United States.* Exhibition catalog. New York: Museum of Modern Art, 1941.

Dubin, Lois Sherr. *The History of Beads: From 30,000 B.C. to the Present.* New York: Abrams, 1987.

————. *North American Indian Jewelry and Adornment: From Prehistory to the Present.* New York: Abrams, 1999.

Eickemeyer, Carl. *Over the Great Navajo Trail.* New York: n.p., 1900.

Ellinger, E. "The Zunis and their jewelry." *Arizona Highways* 28 (August 1952): 8-12.

Erikson, Joan Mowat. *The Universal Bead.* New York: W.W. Norton, 1969; new paperback ed., 1993.

Evetts, Jay, and Robert Ashton. *Southwestern Bandolier Bags from the Evetts and Elkhart Collections.* [Santa Fe]: Elkhart Collection, 1999.

Ewers, John Canfield. "The Emergence of the Named Indian Artist in the American West." *American Indian Art Magazine* 6 (1981): 52-62, 77.

Fane, Diana. *Objects of Myth and Memory: American Indian Art at the Brooklyn Museum.* Brooklyn, NY: Brooklyn Museum of Art, in assoc. with University of Washington Press, 1991.

Farnham, Emily. "Decorative Design in Indian Jewelry." *Design* 35 (March 1934): 13-15, 23-24.

Feder, Norman. *American Indian Art.* New York: Abradale Press, 1995. (Originally published 1971.)

Feest, Christian F. *Native Arts of North America.* London: Thames & Hudson, 1980.

Fewkes, Jesse Walter. *Hopi Katcinas Drawn by Native Artists: Extract from the Twenty-first Annual Report of the Bureau of American Ethnology.* Washington, D.C.: Government Printing Office, 1904.

Fox, Nancy. "Southwest Indian Jewelry." *El Palacio* 93 (summer-fall 1987): 32-34.

————. "Southwestern Indian Jewelry." In Laboratory of Anthropology (Museum of Indian Arts and Culture), *I Am Here: Two Thousand Years of Southwestern Indian Arts and Culture.* Santa Fe: Museum of New Mexico Press, 1989, pp. 61-87.

Frisbie, Theodore R. "Zuni Jewelry and the Engraver's Pencil." *MasterKey* 56 (October-December 1982): 150-152.

Garmhausen, Winona. *History of Indian Arts Education in Santa Fe: The Institute of American Indian Arts, with Historical Background.* Santa Fe: Sunstone Press, 1988.

Gillespie, Alva H. *How to Invest in Indian Jewelry.* Albuquerque: Jackal Jewelry Co., [c. 1974].

Hammack, Nancy S., and Jerry Jacka. *Indian Jewelry of the Prehistoric Southwest.* Tucson: University of Arizona Press, 1975.

Hammons, Lee. *Southwestern Turquoise: The Indians' Skystone.* Glendale: Arizona Maps and Books, 1976.

Harrington, M.R. "Swedged Navaho Bracelets." *Masterkey* 8 (November 1934): 183-184.

Harvey, Brian, E.W. Jernigan, and Gary Witherspoon. *White Metal Universe: Navajo Silver from the Fred Harvey Collection.* Exhibition catalog. Phoenix: Heard Museum, 1981.

Hegemann, Elizabeth C. *Navaho Silver.* Leaflets, no. 29. Los Angeles: Southwest Museum, 1962.

Hersh, Phyllis. "Indian Jewelers of the Southwest." *Exxon USA* 16 (1977): 2-9.

Hill, Gertrude. "The Art of the Navajo Silversmith." *The Kiva* 11 (February 1937): 17-20.

————. "Turquoise and the Zuni Indians." *The Kiva* 12 (May 1947): 43-52.

Hodge, F.W. "How Old Is Southwestern Indian Silverwork?' *El Palacio* 25 (October 1928): 224-232.

————. *Turquoise Found at Hawikuh, New Mexico.* Leaflets, no. 2. New York: Museum of the American Indian, Heye Foundation, 1921.

Hunt, Walter Ben. *Indian Silversmithing.* New York: Bruce Publishing, 1960.

Jacka, Jerry. "Innovations in Southwestern Indian Jewelry: Fine Art in the 1980s." *American Indian Art Magazine* 9 (spring 1984): 28-37.

Jacka, Lois, and Jerry Jacka. *Art of the Hopi: Contemporary Journeys on Ancient Pathways.* Flagstaff: Northland Press, 1998.

————. *Beyond Tradition: Contemporary Indian Art and its Evolution.* Flagstaff: Northland Press, 1988.

————. *Enduring Traditions: Art of the Navajo.* Flagstaff: Northland Press, 1994.

————. *Navajo Jewelry: A Legacy of Silver and Stone.* Flagstaff: Northland Press, 1995.

Jernigan, E.W. *Jewelry of the Prehistoric Southwest.* Santa Fe: School of American Research, 1978.

Karasik, Carol. *The Turquoise Trail: Native American Jewelry and Culture of the Southwest.* New York: Abrams, 1993.

Kenagy, Suzanne G. "'Made in the Zuni Style': Zuni Pueblo and the Arts of the Southwest." *MasterKey* 61 (winter 1988): 11-20.

Kirk, Ruth Falkenburg. *Southwestern Indian Jewelry.* School of American Research. Papers, no. 38. Santa Fe: School of American Research, 1945.

Kramer, William J. *Bola Tie: New Symbol of the West.* Flagstaff: Northland Press, 1978.

Levy, Gordon. *Who's Who in Zuni Jewelry.* Denver: Western Arts Publishing Co., 1980.

Lincoln, Louise, ed. *Southwest Indian Silver from the Doneghy Collection.* Exhibition catalog. Minneapolis: Minneapolis Institute of Arts, 1982.

Mack, John. *Ethnic Jewelry.* New York: Abrams, 1988.

MacManis, Kent. *A Guide to Zuni Fetishes and Carvings.* Tucson: Treasure Chest Books, 1995.

Mangum, Richard, and Sherry Mangum. "The Hopi Silver Project of the Museum of Northern Arizona." *Plateau* n.s., no. 1 (1995): complete issue.

Matthews, Washington. "Navajo Silversmiths." *Second Annual Report to the Smithsonian Institution from the Bureau of Ethnology, 1880-81.* Washington, D.C.: Government Printing Office, 1883, pp. 167-178.

McGibbeny, J.H. "Hopi Jewelry." *Arizona Highways* 26 (July 1950): 18-25.

McGreevy, S.B. "Indian Jewelry of the Southwest: Finished in Beauty." *Art and Antiques* 3 (May-June 1980): 110-117.

Miller, Anna M. "American Indian Jewelry." In her *Gems and Jewelry Appraising: Techniques of Professional Practice.* New York: Van Nostrand Reinhold, 1988, pp. 110-112.

Monongye, Preston. "The New Indian Jewelry Art of the Southwest." *Arizona Highways* 47 (June 1972): 6-11, 46-47.

Monthan, Guy, and Doris Monthan. *Art and Indian Individualists.* Flagstaff: Northland Press, 1975.

Moore, J.B. *The Catalogues of Fine Navajo Blankets, Rugs, Ceremonial Baskets, Silverware, Jewelry and Curios: Originally Published between 1903 and 1911.* Albuquerque: Avanyu Publishing, 1987.

Neumann, David L. "The Indian Jewelry Business." *Masterkey* 38, 2 (1964): 70-73.

————. "Modern Developments in Indian Jewelry." *El Palacio* 57 (June 1950): 175-180.

————. "Navaho Silversmithing Survives." *El Palacio* 50, 1 (January 1943): 6-8.

————. *Navajo Silversmithing.* Santa Fe: Museum of New Mexico, 1971.

Ostler, James, Marian Rodee, and Milford Nahohai. *Zuni, A Village of Silversmiths.* Zuni: A:shiwi Publishing, 1996.

Riodan, M.J. "Navajo Indians." *Overland Monthly* 16 (October 1890): 373-380.

Ritzenthaler, Robert E. "Hopi Indian Silverwork." *Lore* 16 (summer 1966): 92-98.

Roessel, Robert A. *Navajo Arts and Crafts.* Rough Rock, AZ: Navajo Resource Center, Rough Rock Demonstration School, 1982.

Schiffer, Nancy. *Jewelry by Southwest American Indians: Evolving Designs.* West Chester, PA: Schiffer Publishing, 1990.

————. *Turquoise Jewelry.* West Chester, PA: Schiffer Publishing, 1990.

Schiller, Marlene. "Turquoise Jewelry of the Southwest." *Art and Antiques* 6 (September-October 1983): 58-63.

Sides, Dorothy Smith. *Decorative Art of the Southwestern Indians.* New York: Dover, 1961.

Sikorski, K.A. "Recent Trends in Zuni Jewelry." Unpublished M.A. thesis. University of Arizona, Tucson, 1958.

————. "Zuni Jewelry." *Arizona Highways* 35 (August 1959): 6-13.

Slaney, Deborah C. *Blue Gem, White Metal: Carvings and Jewelry from the C.G. Wallace Collection.* Phoenix: Heard Museum, 1998.

————. "The Role of C.G. Wallace in the Development of Twentieth-Century Zuni Silver and Lapidary Arts." M.A. Thesis. University of Oklahoma, Norman, 1992.

Slifer, Dennis, and James Duffield. *Kokopelli: Flute Player Images in Rock Art.* Santa Fe: Ancient City Press, 1994.

Stephen, A.M. "The Navajo." *American Anthropologist* 6 (October 1893): 345-362.

Stevenson, James. *An Illustrated Catalogue of the Collections Obtained from the Indians of New Mexico in 1880.* Washington, D.C.: Government Printing Office, 1883.

————. *An Illustrated Catalogue of the Collections Obtained from the Pueblos of Zuni and Walpi during the Field Season of 1881.* Washington, D.C.: Government Printing Office, 1885.

Tanner, Clara Lee. "Contemporary Southwest Indian Silver." *The Kiva* 25 (February 1960): 1-22.

————. "The Influence of the White Man on Southwest Indian Art." *Ethnohistory* 7 (1960): 137-150.

————. "The Naja." *American Indian Art Magazine* 7 (spring 1982): 64-71.

————. *Prehistoric Southwestern Craft Arts.* Tucson: University of Arizona Press, 1976.

————. "The Squash Blossom." *American Indian Art Magazine* 3 (summer 1978): 36-43.

————. *Southwest Indian Craft Arts.* Tucson: University of Arizona Press, 1968.

————. "Southwestern Indian Gold Jewelry." *The Kiva* 50 (1985): 201-211.

Tryk, Sheila. *Santa Fe Indian Market: Showcase of Native American Art.* Santa Fe: Tierra Publishing, 1993.

Turner, Jane, ed. *The Dictionary of Art.* London: Grove, 1996. See Native North American Art section in vol. 22.

Ullmann, Eleanor E. "The Bola Tie." *Arizona Highways* 42 (October 1966): 2-7.

United States. Census Office. 11th Census. 1890. *Moqui Pueblo Indians of Arizona and Pueblo Indians of New Mexico.* By Thomas Donaldson, Expert Special Agent. Washington, D.C.: U.S. Government Printing Office, 1893.

Vigil, Arnold, ed. *The Allure of Turquoise.* Santa Fe: New Mexico Magazine, 1995.

Volk, Robert M. "Barter, Blankets, and Bracelets: The Role of the Trader in the Navajo Textile and Silverwork Industries, 1868-1930." *American Indian Culture and Research Journal* 12 (1988): 39-63.

Wade, Edwin L., ed. *Arts of the North American Indian: Native Traditions in Evolution.* New York: Hudson Hills Press, 1986.

Wadsworth, Beula. *Design Motifs of the Pueblo Indians: With Applications in Modern Decorative Arts.* San Antonio: Naylor Co., 1957.

Washburn, Dorothy K., ed. *The Elkus Collection: Southwestern Indian Art.* [San Francisco]: California Academy of Sciences; dist. by University of Washington Press, 1984.

With Beauty All Around Me: Art of the Native Southwest. Scottsdale, AZ: Scottsdale Center for the Arts, 1998.

Woodward, Arthur. "'Indian Maid' Jewelry." *Masterkey* 14 (November 1941): 221-224.

————. *Navajo Silver: A Brief History of Navajo Silversmithing.* Flagstaff: Northland Press, 1971, 1973.

————. "Navajo Silver Comes of Age." *Quarterly of the Los Angeles County Museum* 10, 1 (1953): 9-14.

Wright, Margaret Nickelson. *Hopi Silver: The History and Hallmarks of Hopi Silversmithing.* Flagstaff: Northland, 1972; rev. and expanded ed., 1989.

Younger, Erin. *Loloma: A Retrospective View.* Phoenix: The Heard Museum, 1978.

Index

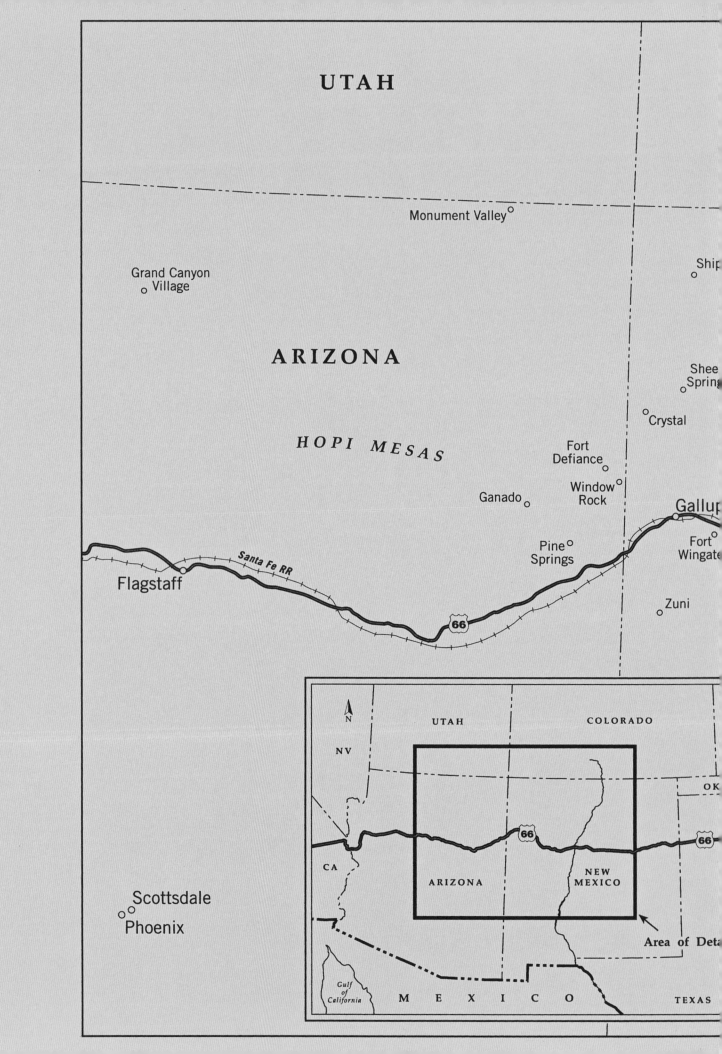

UTAH

Monument Valley °

Ship

Grand Canyon
Village °

ARIZONA

Shee
Spring

Crystal °

HOPI MESAS

Fort
Defiance °

Window °
Rock

Ganado °

Gallup

Santa Fe RR

Pine °
Springs

Fort
Wingate

Flagstaff

66

Zuni °

N

UTAH   COLORADO

NV

OK

CA

66

66

ARIZONA   NEW
               MEXICO

Scottsdale
° °
Phoenix

Area of Det

Gulf
of
California

M E X I C O

TEXAS